MORRIS

COUNTY

BIRTHPLACE OF THE FUTURE

Produced in cooperation with the Morris County Chamber of Commerce.

The Morris County Chamber of Commerce and Community Communications, Inc.,

would like to express our gratitude to these companies for their leadership in the development of this book.

AMERICAN HOME PRODUCTS CORPORATION

GPU

CCM COUNTY COLLEGE of MORRIS

McKinsey&Company

DPC CIRRUS

Morristown Memorial Hospital ATLANTIC HEALTH SYSTEM

Photos by L. A. Popp.

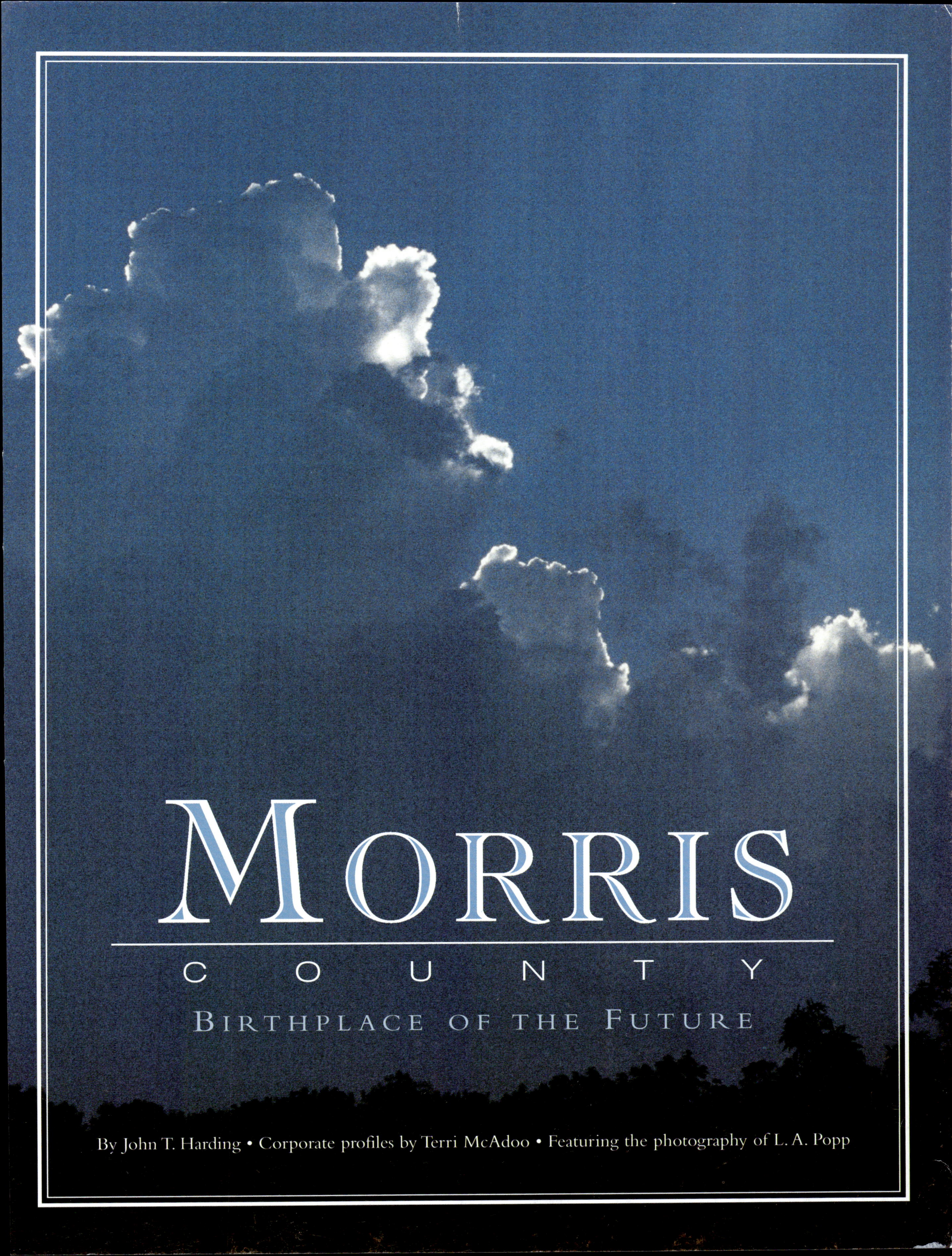

MORRIS
COUNTY
BIRTHPLACE OF THE FUTURE

By John T. Harding • Corporate profiles by Terri McAdoo • Featuring the photography of L. A. Popp

MORRIS
COUNTY

BIRTHPLACE OF THE FUTURE

By John T. Harding
Corporate profiles by Terri McAdoo
Featuring the photography of L. A. Popp

Community Communications, Inc.
Publisher: Ronald P. Beers

Staff for *Morris County: Birthplace of the Future*
Acquisitions: Henry S. Beers
Publisher's Sales Associates: Jim Smith and John Tew
Editor in Chief: Wendi L. Lewis
Managing Editor: Amy Newell
Profile Editor: Amanda J. Burbank
Design Director: Scott Phillips
Designer: Matt Johnson
Photo Editors: Matt Johnson and Amy Newell
Contract Manager: Christi Stevens
National Sales Manager: Bob Sadoski
Sales Assistant: Sandra Akers
Acquisitions Assistant: Angela P. White
Proofreader: Allison L. Griffin
Accounting Services: Stephanie Perez
Print Production Manager: Jarrod Stiff
Pre-Press and Separations:
Artcraft Graphic Productions

CCI
Community Communications, Inc.
Montgomery, Alabama

David M. Williamson, *Chief Executive Officer*
Ronald P. Beers, *President*
W. David Brown, *Chief Operating Officer*

Published 2001
Printed in USA
First Edition
Library of Congress Catalog Number: 00-012449
ISBN: 1-58192-033-4

Photo by L. A. Popp.

Table of Contents

Part One

Part Two

Preface

The start of a new millennium has been celebrated by millions of people around the world, all taking stock of where they are, where they have been, and where they plan to be in future decades. Morris County, New Jersey, is no exception. Yet even though Morris County shares common visions for the new millennium, its opportunities for longtime residents and newcomers are far from ordinary.

Morris County has a remarkable history, of course, but that can be said of many other regions, towns, states, and nations. Morris County has an extraordinary present, also, but that, too, can be said of others. What makes Morris County unique is the way past and present are fused to generate a future that is more than remarkable or extraordinary; its success is practically guaranteed.

This book draws from my own life as a resident of Morris County. I was born here, I grew up here, and I still live here. I have seen many changes as dairy farms become corporate campuses and quiet villages acquire bustling sophistication.

Yet through all the changes, the region's ideals remain—pride in history and hope for the future, in times both good and not so good. As a journalist who has spent more than 30 years watching Morris County's future unfold, I hope you enjoy this view of my home.

—John T. Harding

Photo by L. A. Popp.

Foreword

Trees

By Joyce Kilmer

I think that I shall never see
A poem lovely as a tree.

A tree whose hungry mouth is prest
Against the earth's sweet flowing breast;

A tree that looks at God all day,
And lifts her leafy arms to pray;

A tree that may in Summer wear
A nest of robins in her hair;

Upon whose bosom snow has lain;
Who intimately lives with rain.

Poems are made by fools like me,
But only God can make a tree.

Morris County...Birthplace of the Future. The birthing of this place continues. The men and women whose lives have created our unique 263-year history nurture our passage into the future.

Our ancestors infuse our community with tradition and history while giving us the inspiration to move on. Our freedom from England was secured in part in Morris County by General George Washington, his army and helpful community. As a result, the county and Morristown earned the title "Military Capital of the American Revolution."

Blessed by rich natural resources, the area attracted settlers who used these gifts to create wealth through farming and mining. They stayed. Aided by its natural beauty, Morris County attracted other people who would come here to live and enjoy its mountains, lakes, and greenery.

Evolving into a superb business center for world-class small, medium and global companies, Morris County's workforce became sought after for its creativity, teamwork, and entrepreneurial spirit.

Respect for education, and the wealth to provide it, make Morris County the home of renowned universities, colleges, and schools. From preschool to graduate study, Morris County provides the opportunity for quality global learning.

The quality of life in Morris County is enhanced by premier health-care facilities, a park system that includes public golf courses, museums, restaurants, and an interesting and diverse social life. Nationally recognized theater, symphonies, and art also enhance the culture of our community.

Morris County's culture can be said to be a blend of poetry and nature.

It is like a poem in that it represents the intelligence of men and women applied to the creation of a reality that inspires, educates, and pleases.

It is like a tree because it is a living reality. Our culture grows through the nurturing of its inhabitants. It adapts to the environment and changes its form and direction to sustain its life.

On behalf of the Chamber's Board of Directors, our members and staff, we invite you to walk through this book and to share Morris County with us.

—*Bill Donnelly, President*
Morris County Chamber of Commerce

Kilmer taught in the Morris School District, Morris County, before serving in World War I. From *Joyce Kilmer Volume One, Memoir and Poems,* edited by Robert Cortes Holliday.

Photo by L. A. Popp.

PART ONE

1

A Lasting Legacy

In Morris County, a forward vision ensures the area's growing place in history.

Fall colors blaze along the banks of the Musconetcong River, located on Morris County's western border. Photo by L. A. Popp.

A monument on the grounds of the Ford Mansion and Museum commemorates George Washington's role in the Revolutionary War. The mansion, which served as Washington's headquarters during the war, is part of the Morristown National Historical Park. Photo by L. A. Popp.

The spirit of innovation has been thriving in Morris County for centuries.

Established in 1738-1739, Morris County rose to the forefront during the Revolutionary War when the area served as headquarters for General George Washington. The electromagnetic telegraph was perfected in Morristown in 1838, revolutionizing communications across the globe. Throughout the 20th century, Morris County was home to outstanding technological advances, including development of radio, radar, and computer systems.

Today this same creative spirit continues to thrive throughout the region. For communities and corporations alike, Morris County is a place with sound ideas and ideals—the *Birthplace of the Future.*

In the early years, Morris County supplied a safe haven for the Continental Army during the Revolutionary War.

Morristown, the county seat, is only 30 miles from Manhattan, and strategic posts in the region helped General George Washington track movements of British troops while his own army spent two harsh winters—beginning in January 1777 and again in 1779-80—in the hills and fields nearby.

It was, indeed, a time "to try men's souls," as Thomas Paine wrote. But the memory of those harsh winters is not forgotten by the people of Morris County. While Paine's efforts were commemorated nationwide for nearly 200 years, Morris was the first to erect a statue in his honor. Morristown was long-known as "The Military Capital of the Revolution," and it became home to the nation's first National Historical Park in 1937. The Jockey Hollow army encampment site two miles west of town is the largest portion of the park, with other buildings in town providing key sites of interest.

Among these buildings is the Jacob Ford Mansion, which Washington used as his headquarters during the winter of 1779-80, and which was purchased and preserved by a group of citizens who formed the Washington Association in the mid-19th century. The association turned over the house and grounds to the federal government when the Morristown National Historical Park was formed.

It was from this headquarters after that terrible winter that Washington issued a general order giving the troops a day off to observe St. Patrick's Day, since so many of the soldiers were Irish. This was the first official American observance of the day. Previously, New York City parades were arranged by Irish officers in the British Army.

Nearby is the Schuyler House, where the young Alexander Hamilton, an aide to General Washington, courted Betsy Schuyler. And in the center of town is a plaque marking the site of the first of Benedict Arnold's courts-martial.

But the industrious citizens of Morris County did more than just provide housing, food, and clothing to the rebel army. A powder mill, critical to any army's military success, also was a thriving project not far from the Ford Mansion. It was such a well-kept secret, however, that the exact site of the mill was not located for nearly 200 years, when a plaque was set up in time for the Bicentennial celebrations in 1976.

In addition to powder, iron mines of western Morris County provided military hardware for the army. And the tradition of supplying munitions to the American military continued well into the 20th century, with two powder companies active in Kenvil, and an arsenal and research and development center at Picatinny, both near Dover.

In the early 19th century, the Morris Canal was dug to bring coal from Pennsylvania by barge to the burgeoning manufacturing cities of Paterson, Newark, and Jersey. The project was organized and led by George P. Macculloch of Morristown, whose former home now is open to the public.

Lake Hopatcong, the largest lake in New Jersey, was created as a water source for the system of locks that brought the canal barges over the hills and mountains of western New Jersey. And when the railroads came, the lake quickly became a prized recreation area, as boats ferried vacationers from the railroad station at the southern end of the lake to the resort hotels that ringed 26 miles of shoreline.

But Morris County never rests on the laurels of its early history. For more than two centuries, Morris County has led the nation in technological innovation. The tradition that began during the Revolutionary War continued in the early 19th century at the Speedwell Iron Works in Morristown, the most advanced manufacturing facility in the nation at the time. It was here that the boiler for the steamship *Savannah*, the first to cross the Atlantic under its own power, was made.

A few years later, in 1837, Samuel F. B. Morse brought the working model of his telegraph to Morristown, where it was perfected by Alfred Vail, son of the owner of the Speedwell Iron Works. And in the 19th century, another family member, Theodore Vail, merged several small, competing communications firms to organize the American Telephone and Telegraph Co.

Throughout Morris County, technological advances continue. Boonton has long been a center for aircraft radio technology, with companies involved in research, development, and production of radio and radar communications.

Bell Labs, now a division of Lucent Technologies, holds hundreds of patents in many areas of telecommunications research. The company's facility in Whippany, as well as the main research center in Murray Hill, leads the nation in technology research. The transistor was developed by the Bell Labs staff, as well as the Unix computer operating system.

Technology, however, is not the only source of pride for Morris County. Joyce Kilmer, author of the poem "Trees," taught at Morristown High School before leaving for military service in World War I. And, Thomas Nast, the political cartoonist who first drew the Democratic donkey and the GOP elephant, lived in Morristown for 40 years. It was Nast who also gave the nation its modern portrait of Santa Claus.

The first American guide dogs for the blind were trained at The Seeing Eye, which still maintains its headquarters in Morristown. The dogs, their trainers, and the people they serve can be observed regularly on the streets of Morristown during training sessions.

Morris County maintains pride in the past, but its people also look to the future. Careful zoning plans have set aside thousands of acres for parklands to ensure a quality environment for generations to come. Those same plans include room for commercial growth; other areas allocated for office and industrial use utilize the county's transportation links to major metropolitan regions throughout the Northeast. In Morris County, a forward vision ensures the area's growing place in history. □

The Abbey, constructed in 1904, was home to several prominent Morristown families. The building now serves as headquarters for The Private Bank. Photo by L. A. Popp.

Visitors to Morristown National Historical Park explore reconstructed Revolutionary War huts in Jockey Hollow. Soldiers took shelter in similar wooden structures during the bitter winter of 1779-80. Photo by L. A. Popp.

Many churches throughout Morris County have served their communities for centuries. Photo by L. A. Popp.

Residents and visitors can find many avenues to experience the charm of Morris County's early days. Photo by L. A. Popp.

Historic Speedwell is home to the factory where Alfred Vail and Samuel F. B. Morse perfected the telegraph in 1838. Photos by L. A. Popp.

After a tour of Historic Speedwell, visitors can cross Route 202 and relax along the banks of Speedwell Lake, one of many public parks maintained by the Town of Morristown.

Waterloo Village's history dates back more than three centuries, when the area was home to the Lenape tribe. During the early days of white settlement, Waterloo was a part of Morris County, which covered a larger area. In later years, the village became part of Sussex County and prospered during the heyday of the Morris Canal. Today, Waterloo Village is open to the public, and visitors can tour a reconstructed Lenape village, as well as many historic homes. Photos by L. A. Popp.

Morris County remains home to descendants of Native Americans who lived in the area centuries ago. Each June, the Nanticoke Lenni-Lenape Indians of New Jersey hold an annual pow-wow in the area, and the public is invited to share in the rich culture of these tribes. Photos by L. A. Popp.

The Bloch Brothers building, a Dover landmark, is home to a weekly antique auction. Photo by L. A. Popp.

Indoors and out, area antique shops hold keepsakes to complement any decor. Photos by L. A. Popp.

Photos by L. A. Popp.

American Home Products Corporation

American Home Products (AHP) has a long history of exploring and addressing human and animal health-care needs. Along the way, AHP has built a legacy for sharing its expertise and financial success with organizations that support health care, education, the arts, business and civic activities, and social services. Each year, AHP employees volunteer many hours supporting outreach agencies like the United Way, and the corporation provides funding and product donations for organizations that help people lead healthier and happier lives.

County College of Morris

The County College of Morris generously shares its knowledge and resources with the community. Annually, 50,000 people visit the college to cheer at sporting events, savor fine arts programs, and sample a wealth of on-campus lectures. Off campus, the college provides guest speakers to schools and other community sites to talk about topics of interest and importance to the community. The college is visible in the business community, too, providing tailored programs that help local businesses strengthen their workforce.

DPC Cirrus Inc.

At DPC Cirrus, ingenuity is changing health care around the world. The company designs, develops, manufactures, and services an automated line of immunoassay analyzers, known as IMMULITE® and IMMULITE 2000. These high-tech instruments enable clinical laboratories to provide quick and accurate test results for a variety of diseases, such as allergy, thyroid function, diabetes, infectious diseases, reproductive disorders, and cancer. The result: Doctors are diagnosing and treating patients within hours instead of days.

Photos by L. A. Popp.

GPU, Inc.

Over the past few years, GPU, Inc., has been redefining its business to capitalize on the changes transforming the industry. As it enters new businesses, such as telecommunications and utilities construction, and forges stronger partnerships, GPU holds fast to its commitment to customer and community service. Collectively, the company invests millions of dollars in customer service; individually, employees dedicate thousands of hours to support nonprofit groups, schools, and community organizations that help adults and children live happier and healthier lives.

McKINSEY & COMPANY

Over the past 70 years, McKinsey & Company has made a deeper impact on business than any management consulting firm in the world. The diversity within McKinsey's ranks enables the firm to embrace a range of clients and needs, from large companies grappling with organizational change, to new businesses struggling with e-commerce, to non-profits raising awareness about teenage addiction. Through its integrated global network of teams with deep industry knowledge, McKinsey helps clients achieve positive, lasting change that delivers higher performance and develops stronger business leaders for the future.

MORRISTOWN MEMORIAL HOSPITAL— ATLANTIC HEALTH SYSTEM

Improving community health is at the core of services provided by Atlantic Health System's Morristown Memorial Hospital. Hospital leaders identify the health issues in the area and collaborate with local organizations to develop programs that build healthier communities. The staff, physicians, nurses, and volunteers give generously of their time, resources, and expertise. As a result, each year thousands of people of all ages benefit from free health screenings, educational programs, free and low-cost immunizations, and an interactive health-care Web site for teens.

Photos by L. A. Popp.

4420
NJ TRANSIT

2

Morris County Today

As the new millennium begins, very different groups are working in unison to shape Morris County's future.

Morris County is well served by public transportation. Currently, three New Jersey Transit commuter rail lines run through the county, making stops at the county's eighteen stations. Photo by L. A. Popp.

Lucent Technologies, located at the International Trade Center in Mount Olive, is one of the top employers in Morris County. Photo by L. A. Popp.

The real value of any nation, as Adam Smith pointed out in his 1776 book, *The Wealth of Nations*, is its people. And in Morris County, the value of the people is enriched by their diversity, both culturally and socially.

Morris County, with a total land area of 469 square miles, has a population of approximately 460,000, up from 421,361 as counted in the 1990 Census. By the year 2010, some 485,000 people will call Morris County home. The 1990 Census indicated five percent of the population was Hispanic, but that number has been growing substantially. About another five percent claimed Asian descent, with nearly an equal number of African Americans. The census showed a balance of male and female residents.

Some 10,000 people commute to jobs in New York City, about 30 miles away, while another 27,000 travel to Newark and other Essex County locations for their jobs. Most, however—some 140,000—both live and work in Morris County.

Although Morris County lies on the western fringe of the megalopolis that stretches from Boston to Washington, careful community planning has maintained a balance between development and open space. As a result, the quality of both residential and business life has flourished, and the towns of Morris County, including Morristown, Dover, and Boonton, as well as the many boroughs and townships, are thriving.

Nabisco corporate headquarters are located in Parsippany, New Jersey. The company is one of the strongest food brands in the U.S., with a line of products including Oreos, Chips Ahoy!, Ritz Crackers, Newtons, and many other cookies and crackers. The company is a subsidiary of RJR/ Nabisco. Photo by L. A. Popp.

Visitors to the area on business or pleasure can find luxury accommodations at the Headquarters Plaza Hotel in Morristown, close to downtown, historic sites, shopping, and restaurants. Photo by L. A. Popp.

Bargain hunters are drawn to the flea market on Blackwell Street in Dover, where dozens of vendors display wares ranging from fresh flowers to hand-me-downs. The flea market truly proves the adage that "one man's trash is another's treasure." Photo by L. A. Popp.

In recent years, Morris County has changed from a labor-intensive agricultural and industrial market to a high-technology and capital-intensive region, peopled by workers with higher entrepreneurial skills, more education, and greater expertise in technology.

The largest employers in the county are in the fields of technology and health care. AT&T Corp. and Lucent Technologies together employ more than 10,000, hospitals account for another 8,000 jobs, and three major pharmaceutical firms provide some 7,000 positions.

With jobs like this, high incomes can be expected: Per capita income rose from $9,909 in 1979 to $25,177 in 1989, according to statistics compiled by the Morris County Planning Board. And median family income is more than $62,000—one of the highest levels in the United States.

Residents also enjoy educational advantages. With three universities and a two-year community college in Morris County, as well as easy access to many other colleges and universities in northern New Jersey, the people of Morris County are among the nation's best educated.

Economic growth during the last half of the 20th century has transformed Morris County from a largely rural area to one of suburban housing and office parks. But outward growth has been accompanied by a revival of town centers; instead of commuting, many younger residents want to live within walking distance of their jobs, shops and restaurants, and social activities. Parents and grandparents—the "empty nesters"—increasingly are choosing the city life as well, selling bigger suburban homes on large lots and relocating in urban centers. In turn, affordable suburban houses are available for newcomers to Morris County as corporations follow staffers from the big city bustle to suburban office sites.

Morris County also has attracted thousands of the country's newest citizens. These recent arrivals are expanding the area's work force and filling a wide variety of jobs from industrial to high-tech positions. And the new wave of immigration adds to the cultural mix that has long been a hallmark of the region.

Moreover, this ethnic diversity is adding life to the county's urban areas. Blackwell Street in Dover, Main Street in Boonton, and Speedwell Avenue in Morristown are thriving once again as new residents help to revitalize once-neglected neighborhoods. Their efforts, coupled with government-sponsored Urban Renewal programs, have created a hub of activity on streets that were formerly barren and dreary. Along a single street in Morristown, Dover, or Boonton, a variety of restaurants and shops reflect such diverse cultures as Asian, Brazilian, Salvadoran, Colombian, Caribbean, Afghan, and Indian, as well as those who arrived in the previous immigration wave — Italian, Irish, Jewish, and German.

Old and young, longtime residents and newcomers, urban dwellers and suburbanites—all add to the cultural kaleidoscope that comprises Morris County. As the new millennium begins, these very different groups are working in unison to shape Morris County's future. ☐

Morris County encompasses a cultural kaleidoscope of diverse nationalities, varying ages, newcomers to the area and those who have lived here their whole lives through. Together, they create a vibrant community full of the joy of life. Photos by L. A. Popp.

With twenty-five county parks on over 13,300 acres, four state parks, a national historic park, and a national wildlife refuge, Morris County has made a strong commitment to the preservation of open space. The county even features an Adopt-A-Trail program for the preservation of hiking and walking trails throughout the area. Photos by L. A. Popp.

Morris County's high quality of life is the result of careful developmental planning. Residents enjoy green spaces and room for recreation even in the heart of downtown areas. Photos by L. A. Popp.

Above left: In 1894, the Boonton Library moved to the former home of James Holmes on Main Street. Holmes willed the property to the town in 1893 for use as a library. Photo by L. A. Popp.

Above right: Quaint antique shops and other specialty shops are located around the Main Street area of Boonton.

Left: The friendly children's bookseller is still a fixture in Chester, which celebrated its 200th birthday in 1999. Photos by L. A. Popp.

Along a single street in Morristown, Dover, or Boonton, a variety of restaurants and shops reflect such diverse cultures as Asian, Brazilian, Salvadoran, Columbian, Caribbean, Afghan, and Indian, as well as those who arrived in the previous wave of immigration—Italian, Irish, Jewish, and German. Photo by L. A. Popp.

WELCOME

3

Diverse People, Picturesque Places

No matter where they go in Morris County, residents are sure to find a unique blend of history, prosperity, and growth.

People from all walks of life enjoy browsing through Dover's flea market every Sunday. Photo by L. A. Popp.

Of the 44 municipalities in Morris County, three—Morristown, Dover, and Boonton—are incorporated as towns; the rest are boroughs or townships, a remnant of the days when the population was much smaller and most of the region was farmland or forest. Today, however, some formerly rural townships have larger populations than the towns, partly because more land was available for development. But as Morris County enters the new millennium, revitalization of the towns is taking place as many people return to the convenience of an urban lifestyle.

Morristown, the county seat and the largest of the three towns, is only two miles square, with a resident population of 18,000. During the day, however, another 50,000 people arrive in town to work, providing a market for restaurants and retailers of all types. Moreover, many of these commuters stay through the evening to socialize. A summer night can find dozens of people strolling around The Green, a park in the center of town, and enjoying dinner at one of many nearby restaurants. Whether diners want traditional North American cuisine, Italian, Mexican, Colombian, Ecuadorean, Brazilian, Chinese, Thai, or Afghan fare, any can be found within a short walk of the town center.

Dover, with a population of 15,000, also has many multicultural activities, predominantly Hispanic. The cultural influx has reinvigorated both Dover neighborhoods and shops along Blackwell Street, Dover's main thoroughfare.

Live performances featuring Hispanic music groups have returned to the historic Baker Ballroom at one end of Blackwell Street. And Blackwell is the site of a massive flea market every Sunday that attracts dealers and customers from New Jersey and nearby states. The flea market started three decades ago in a field in nearby Chester, but when the land was sold, the market was moved to downtown Dover, where it continues to thrive.

Morristown's downtown area blends historic scenery with quaint shops and a variety of restaurants. Photos by L. A. Popp.

Boonton, population 8,300, is known as "the town that was moved uphill from rising waters" of the Jersey City Reservoir. The town's winding Main Street satisfies strollers and shoppers alike with its early 20th century architecture and charming antique and craft stores.

For those seeking the ambience of a 19th-century town, the little borough of Chester offers a five-block Main Street lined with artisan shops and anchored with fine restaurants. Chester itself serves as an "anchor" for one end of Route 24 as it threads its two-lane way through Morris County. At the eastern end, however, part of the road has been replaced by a multi-lane, limited-access highway that carries travelers swiftly to nearby metropolitan centers.

Just off this new Route 24 lie Madison and Chatham, two boroughs that are collaborating on a creative community adult school program. The program's innovative offerings include courses such as Native American Healing Ceremonies as Seen through the Eyes of a Modern Surgeon, Introduction to the Irish Language, and Exotic Vegetarian Cuisine of India.

Madison is named "The Rose City" and earned this distinction in the early 1900s for its abundance of flower growers, predominantly from Italy. And Chatham is a treasure of 18th-century homes, a legacy of its pre-Revolutionary War prosperity. Today many of these houses are owned by commuters who work in New York's financial district.

Other municipalities in Morris County offer a contrast with older towns and boroughs. These townships were agricultural and rural areas as recently as 1960, but they now contain office campuses and suburban housing regions. At the same time, neighborhoods still retain many of the wooded areas and open fields that attracted corporations and homeowners in the first place.

Parsippany-Troy Hills, for example, was largely agricultural land and dairy farms only 40 years ago. Today, a modern office campus and Hilton hotel occupy former pastureland at the intersection of Routes 10 and 202. Mount Olive Township, home of the Budd Lake resort area where nationally known Big Bands played in the 1930s and 1940s, now boasts an International Trade Center that houses major corporations.

From urban amenities to suburban comforts, the area's towns and boroughs reflect a variety of lifestyles. No matter where they go, however, Morris residents are sure to find a unique blend of history, prosperity, and growth. ◻

The streets and shops of Dover hold a trove of collectible treasures. Photos by L. A. Popp.

An excellent network of trains serves commuters throughout the area. Photo by L. A. Popp.

Many cultures converge in Morris County, and the mix of nationalities fosters an artistic atmosphere. Photo by L. A. Popp.

The Borough of Madison features a thriving downtown business district. Photo by L. A. Popp.

The International Trade Center in Mount Olive is one of the largest business parks in New Jersey. The 670-acre site includes offices, manufacturing and distribution facilities, and a full-service hotel. Photo by L. A. Popp.

The county's many downtown communities provide wonderful places for families to stroll, shop, and simply relax. Photo by L. A. Popp.

Above: Chester Borough's Volunteer Fire Department has served residents since 1921. Right: Chester's downtown area features an array of antique stores and other unique shops. Photos by L. A. Popp.

Quaint ambiance and architecture are hallmarks of Chester. Photos by L. A. Popp.

Whether the preference is palatial or cozy, Morris County residents can find a home perfectly suited for their lifestyle. Photos by L. A. Popp.

4

A Place to Learn and Live Well

Morris County residents enjoy an enviable lifestyle—a fact enhanced by the area's top-notch educational and medical facilities.

The College of Saint Elizabeth, founded in 1899, features striking architecture and a 200-acre campus. Since its inception, the college has awarded degrees to nearly 10,000 students. Photo by L. A. Popp.

In Morris County, excellent choices abound, and education and health-care services are no exception. Public and private schools provide a firm foundation for further studies, while the area's institutions of higher learning feature a variety of degrees and programs. And two hospital systems offer residents comprehensive, quality care throughout the county.

Three major four-year institutions are located in Morris County near Madison—Drew University, Fairleigh Dickinson University, and the College of Saint Elizabeth. In addition, students can attend the two-year County College of Morris in Randolph, the county-run Vocational-Technical School in Denville, and the privately run Dover Business College.

With a total enrollment of 2,300 students, the highly respected Drew University focuses on liberal arts education but maintains a strong belief in the importance of technology. The school has established an extensive network of computers throughout campus and was named one of America's Most Wired Colleges 2000 by *Yahoo! Life Internet* magazine.

Nearby is the Florham-Madison campus of Fairleigh Dickinson University, which opened in 1958 on an estate created 60 years earlier by one of America's richest couples—Hamilton Twombly and his wife, the former Florence Vanderbilt. Today, FDU focuses on business education courses, with a strong liberal arts emphasis. More than 2,200 undergraduates and 1,500 graduate students attend classes on the Florham-Madison campus.

Next to FDU is the College of Saint Elizabeth, chartered in 1900 as the first four-year Catholic college for women. Today, more than 1,800 full- and part-time students are enrolled in three programs: the Women's College, Adult Undergraduate Degree Programs, and Graduate Programs.

Since its inception in 1968, the County College of Morris has graduated 30,000 students from its 66 degree and certificate programs. Moreover, almost 75 percent of CCM students transfer to four-year institutions to complete their degrees. Full- and part-time enrollment exceeds 7,500, and agreements with 42 colleges and universities make it easy to transfer for a bachelor's degree.

Together, these schools offer the wide range of courses needed to train the growing population of workers seeking jobs in Morris County. From auto mechanics to computer programming to arts and literature, the learning opportunities are almost limitless.

What's more, these learning opportunities begin in the grade school years; municipalities throughout Morris County long ago embraced the state constitution's mandate for "a thorough and efficient" system of public school education. More than 75,000 students in grades K-12 are enrolled in Morris County's public schools, while dozens of private schools and academies offer other educational alternatives.

Institutes of learning are important in Morris County, but facilities that promote better living are just as vital. Throughout the area, medical professionals maintain a strong reputation for providing residents with the best of care.

County College of Morris, a publicly supported two-year school, grants more associate degrees than any community college in the state. Photo by L. A. Popp.

Approximately 7,500 students attend classes at County College of Morris. The school offers 66 degree and certificate programs. Photos courtesy of County College of Morris.

Throughout Morris County, excellent public and private schools provide young students with a solid foundation for further studies. Photo by L. A. Popp.

The Seeing Eye, located in Morristown, trains specially bred dogs to serve as guides for blind men and women. Since 1929, the organization's guide dog program has benefited more than 6,000 individuals. Photos by L. A. Popp.

Two major hospital groups provide health care in Morris County: Atlantic Health System and Saint Clare's Health Services. Each is a consortium of formerly independent hospitals, which creates a more efficient system of care and preserves the presence of smaller community hospitals.

Atlantic Health System operates Morristown Memorial Hospital, a 560-bed facility with specialties such as cancer care, open-heart surgery, critical care, and rehabilitation. Atlantic runs an 11-county network of hospitals in New Jersey, and nearby members include Overlook Hospital in Summit, Mountainside Hospital in Montclair/Glen Ridge, and the General Hospital Center at Passaic.

St. Clare's Health Services serves residents of western Morris County from its main hospital in Denville, and affiliated hospitals are located in Dover, Boonton, and Sussex County. St. Clare's is the New Jersey affiliate of the world-renowned Sloan-Kettering Cancer Center, and it has more than 700 physicians on its staff.

Morris County residents enjoy an enviable lifestyle—a fact enhanced by the area's top-notch educational and medical facilities. Comparable services could be found in major cities, but in Morris, quality schools and health care are always minutes from home. □

More than 2,200 undergraduates and 1,500 graduate students are enrolled at Fairleigh Dickinson University's Florham-Madison campus. FDU is located on the former country estate of early 20th-century socialites Hamilton Twombly and his wife, the former Florence Vanderbilt. Top left photo by L. A. Popp. Other photos courtesy of Fairleigh Dickinson University.

Drew University, located five minutes from Morristown, enjoys a reputation for educational excellence and state-of-the-art computer technology. The independent university has an enrollment of 2,300 students. Photos courtesy of Drew University.

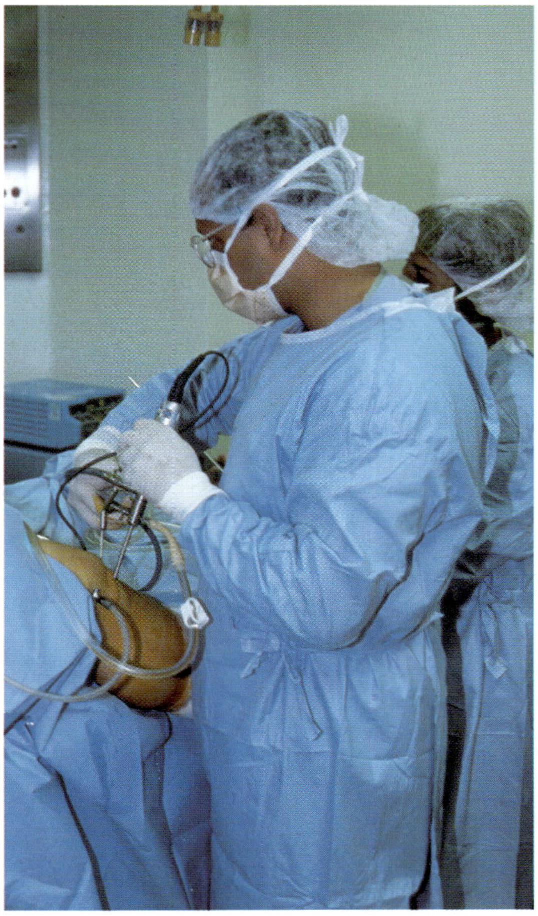

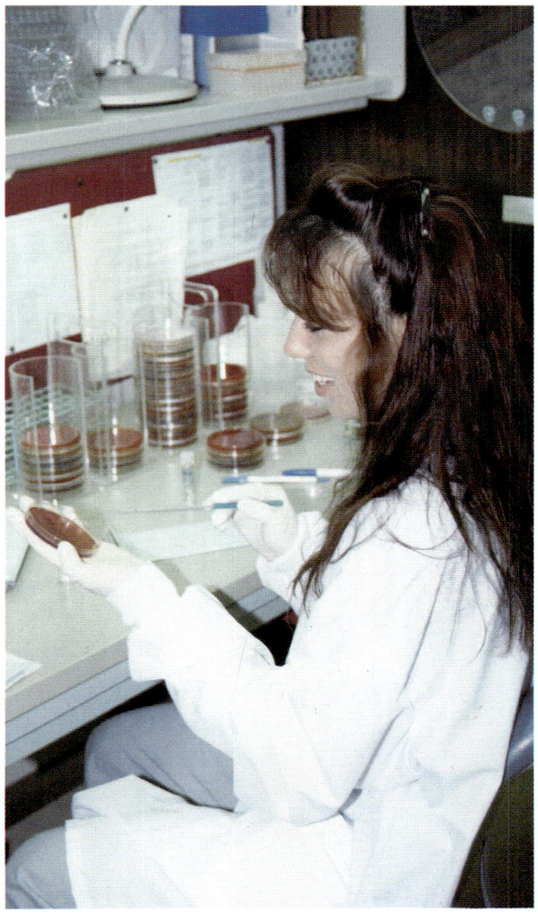

Two major health systems, Atlantic Health System and Saint Clare's Health Services, provide quality care to Morris County residents. Morristown Memorial Hospital, below, is located on Madison Avenue. Photos by L. A. Popp.

5

A Wealth of Art and Adventure

The variety of pastimes found in Morris County, enhanced by local and international traditions, creates a cultural environment usually reserved for big cities.

Spring and summer months bring a variety of outdoor art festivals and exhibits to communities throughout Morris County. Photo by L. A. Popp.

When it's time for leisure, residents can find a world of opportunities in Morris County. Art, theater, and music thrive throughout the area. And for outdoor enthusiasts, the area's superb parks provide the perfect atmosphere for recreational getaways.

From fine art to festivals, Shakespeare to musicals, classical to hip-hop, the cultural scene in Morris County offers selections to please any preference. Fans can enjoy first-rate art, theater, and music, not only from touring artists but from home-grown talent as well.

"Artists live here, and people understand that the quality is here, and they don't want to travel," according to Carolyn Ward, executive director of the Arts Council of the Morris Area.

Nor do they have to. Rather than trek to Manhattan, residents of Morris County can, in many cases, walk to cultural venues. And if they go by car, drivers will find plenty of safe, convenient, and inexpensive or free parking.

Summer brings outdoor art exhibits and cultural festivals to the sidewalks and streets of Morris County, including a Greek Festival in Randolph and Hispanic celebrations in Morristown and Dover. Entertaining events continue during the cooler months as well. New Year's Eve brings the annual First Night Morris celebration, with performances throughout the center of Morristown. And the town's annual St. Patrick's Day Parade draws a large crowd of spectators and marchers from throughout the county.

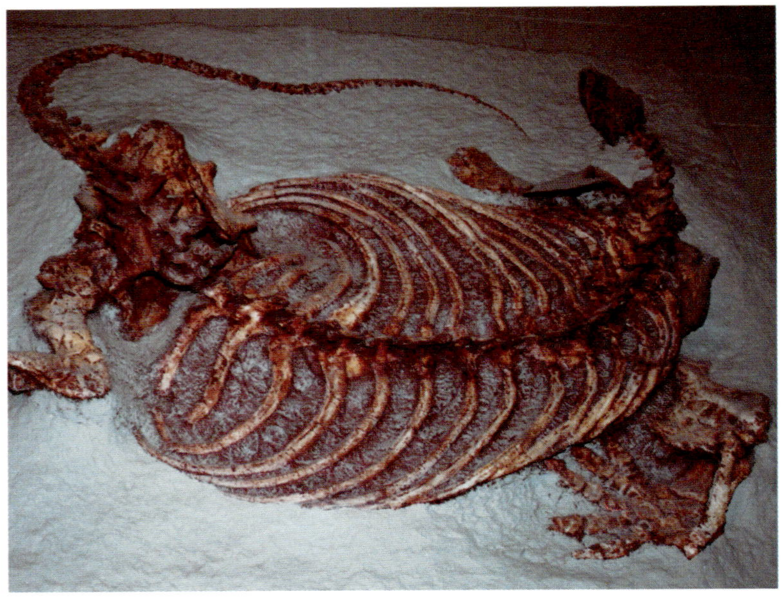

One of New Jersey's leading cultural institutions, the Morris Museum, is located in Morristown. The museum is the state's third largest and attracts more than 300,000 visitors annually. Smaller special interest museums include the Museum of Early Trades and Crafts in Madison and Craftsman Farms, former home of designer Gustav Stickley, in Parsippany.

Thousands of natural and man-made treasures are on display at the Morris Museum, the state's third largest museum. Photos by L. A. Popp.

Another artistic highlight is the Morristown CraftMarket, which is held at least twice a year. Several hundred artisans from throughout the East showcase their work at the CraftMarket's juried exhibition.

Theater fans flock to the New Jersey Shakespeare Festival, a professional independent repertory troupe in residence on the campus of Drew University in Madison. The Festival is Morris County's largest theater company and draws 75,000 people to performances each year. In addition, the refurbished Community Theatre in Morristown features internationally known artists and troupes. Other theatrical groups now grace the stages of refurbished vaudeville houses in towns such as Boonton, Dover, and Netcong, and community theater groups of professional caliber put on productions throughout the county.

Cultural trends continue to move toward community activities, but the Internet also is playing an increasing role. "We recognize the need to make ourselves available to schools, students, and parents via our Web site," says Steven Klindt, executive director of the Morris Museum, "but we also need to make it easy and efficient to come in person."

For those willing to travel, nationally known venues such as the Paper Mill Playhouse in Millburn and the New Jersey Performing Arts Center in Newark are less than an hour's drive away. And since Morris County sits on the fringe of the greater New York metropolitan area, even more cultural events are within easy reach.

For outdoor pursuits, Morris County is filled with open space for parkland recreation use. Residents have always realized history's link to the present and future. As a result, a system of national, state, county, and municipal parks blankets Morris County with green spaces.

The Community Theatre, on South Street in Morristown, is a shining example of how Morris County residents support arts and culture. The structure once sat abandoned and in disrepair, but volunteer efforts led to the theater's restoration. Since 1994, audiences have flocked to The Community Theatre to enjoy music, theater, and dance performances. Photo by L. A. Popp.

Handiwork of early settlers is on display at the Museum of Early Trades and Crafts in downtown Madison. The museum's home, a century-old Romanesque Revival building, was restored to its former glory in the 1990s. Photo by L. A. Popp.

One of the largest parks is the 1,700-acre Morristown National Historical Park, a mostly wooded area two miles west of Morristown. During the Revolutionary War, the Continental Army was stationed at the site and endured two winter seasons—one more severe than the infamous winter at Valley Forge in Pennsylvania. The park also includes the Ford Mansion, headquarters for General George Washington during that bitter winter of 1779-1780.

Adjacent to Morristown National Historical Park is the county-owned Lewis Morris Park. Both parks feature walking and riding trails, but Lewis Morris also has many open fields for sports and picnics, as well as a lake for swimming.

Even larger is the Great Swamp National Wildlife Refuge, with miles of trails and walkways that enable visitors to get "up close and personal" with a variety of wildlife species. In an opposite corner of Morris County—in the mountainous northwest region—are ski resort areas and lakes. Budd Lake, the largest natural lake in New Jersey, is located here, as well as Lake Hopatcong, a man-made lake with 26 miles of shoreline. Lake Hopatcong was created in the early 19th century to provide water for the Morris Canal, a waterway that ran from the Pennsylvania border to Newark. And the county park system includes golf courses, a riding stable, and the William G. Mennen Sports Arena, home of ice rinks, circuses, and arts, crafts, and antiques shows.

The variety of pastimes found in Morris County, enhanced by local and international traditions, creates a cultural environment usually reserved for big cities. Yet here it is—all in Morris County. □

BARRY
TEA
Ireland

Artwork of all styles and sizes fills the streets of downtown during Denville's springtime art festival. Dozens of area artists participate in the event. Photos by L. A. Popp.

The New Jersey Shakespeare Festival attracts approximately 75,000 theater-goers to its productions each year. The festival's new facility, the F. M. Kirby Shakespeare Theatre, is on the campus of Drew University. Photos courtesy of the New Jersey Shakespeare Festival.

Morris County offers an abundance of scenic spots for recreation and relaxation. Photos by L. A. Popp.

Fans of water sports find a perfect summertime playground at Lake Hopatcong. A popular state park and historical museum are located on the lake in Landing. Photos by L. A. Popp.

Art festivals set a colorful scene on The Green in historic downtown Morristown. Photos by L. A. Popp.

A variety of summer concerts are held every year in Waterloo, located just across the Morris-Sussex county line. Photos by L. A. Popp.

Budweiser
NEWS 12
NEW JERSEY

TRAVEL
202

6

A Promising Future

History resonates strongly in the heart of Morris County, and its people share a common vision—one of continuing progress and prosperity.

Like towns and boroughs throughout the county, Morristown supports a thriving business community and still retains a rich historic identity. Photo by L. A. Popp.

Morris County is building on its heritage; while residents preserve their history, they also look ahead eagerly as the new millennium begins. The people of Morris County are preparing for the future, even as they continue to learn from the past.

Since its founding, Morris County has successfully managed change with this combined sense of history and focus on planning. As the trends of recent years continue, residents are certain to see more changes and face some challenges as well.

With the area's growing urbanization, planners remain dedicated to balancing development with preservation of the area's open spaces. Maintaining the blend of urban and rural life that its citizens prefer is a primary goal in Morris.

Today, as the second-wealthiest county in the nation, Morris County's richness is not limited to material assets, but also encompasses its people and its culture. The landscape that is Morris County holds many fields of opportunity, and to ensure the richest harvest, all hands in the county—those from government, business, education, art, culture, medical, and professional—work together.

What's more, those hands will come from increasingly diverse sources, both generational and ethnic. Dr. James Hughes, dean of the Edward Bloustein School of Planning and Public Policy at Rutgers University, notes that people born during the Baby Boom years are maturing adults now, and soon will be senior citizens. In addition, shifting immigration patterns brought new elements of ethnic diversity to Morris County as the 20th century ended. "We don't have to invent our demographic future; it's already in place," according to Hughes.

The ability to be flexible, vital to Morris County's past, will hold equal precedence in the future as demographics shift.

Communities must continue to foster ties beween residents and to recognize that diverse groups are interwoven economically, culturally, and socially.

The future is bringing swift economic changes as well. Research, health-care, and pharmaceutical businesses are moving to the forefront as manufacturing concerns decline. Commercial real estate reaches skyward to conserve available land, and older buildings are undergoing revitalization. Residential construction is shifting to high-density, in-town neighborhoods rather than large-plot rural and suburban ones.

In short, Morris County, birthplace of so many future-changing events in the past 250 years, remains at the forefront of new trends and technologies. History resonates strongly in the heart of Morris County, and its people share a common vision—one of continuing progress and prosperity. □

From modern corporate office parks to quaint downtown streets, Morris County is filled with an attractive atmosphere of prosperity. Photos by L. A. Popp.

ART GLASS STUDIO

Pub
Collins
Collins' Pub
LOBSTE
Collins' Pub
STEAK

Travelers for business and pleasure will find superb accommodations throughout the area. The Hilton Parsippany features more than 500 rooms. Photo by L. A. Popp.

The Ford Mansion, right, and Acorn Hall, far right, are two of Morris County's best-known historic structures. The mansion was headquarters for General George Washington during the Revolutionary War and is now a part of the National Parks System. Acorn Hall, a Victorian mansion designed in the Italianate style, is home to the Morris County Historical Society. Photos by L. A. Popp.

Above: At Historic Speedwell, Morris County residents are remembered for their vital role in America's Industrial Revolution. Right: A monument in downtown Morristown pays tribute to soldiers who defended their country during the Civil War. Photos by L. A. Popp.

Headquarters for the Women's Club of Morristown was built by Dr. Lewis Condict in 1797. The club has maintained the building for more than 50 years. Photo by L. A. Popp.

Morris County's excellent system of parks beckons locals and visitors to the great outdoors. Photos by L. A. Popp.

At work and at play, Morris County residents share a common bond—enduring pride in their communities. Photos by L. A. Popp.

BLAZE

4420
4420
TRANSIT

Photo by L. A. Popp.

Part Two

7

Networks

Photo by Suzanne McGrane.

GPU, Inc.

When deregulation became a fact in New Jersey and Pennsylvania late in the 1990s, it changed the electric utilities industry as never before. Foreseeing those changes, GPU positioned itself to be a more competitive company poised for growth in the deregulated world.

GPU, Inc., is a registered public utility holding company that provides utility and utility-related services to more than six million customers worldwide. GPU is based in

Supporting communities is a way of life at GPU. To assist the American Red Cross in dealing with natural disasters, GPU is donating nine disaster response trailers for use in New Jersey and Pennsylvania communities through 2001.

Morristown and has a number of worldwide subsidiaries, the largest of which is GPU Energy. GPU Energy serves about two million customers directly through three electric companies: Jersey Central Power & Light Company (JCP&L), serving customers in 13 New Jersey counties, and Metropolitan Edison Company (Met-Ed) and Pennsylvania Electric Company (Penelec), serving customers in 44 Pennsylvania counties.

As this book was published, GPU had agreed to merge with FirstEnergy Corp., a diversified energy services holding company in Akron, Ohio. FirstEnergy provides electricity and natural gas services to customers in northern and central Ohio and western Pennsylvania.

"FirstEnergy is the right fit for us in terms of its strategic objectives, our culture and values, our locations, and our systems," says Fred Hafer, chairman, president, and CEO of GPU.

The merger is expected to create the nation's sixth largest investor-owned electric system, based on customers served. It is anticipated that the union will enhance earnings growth potential and revenue opportunities for the combined companies and offer substantial synergies from combining operations.

In its own core domestic electricity delivery business, GPU has undertaken a massive initiative to improve and expand customer service and reduce the cost of providing that service. "Our strategy is to focus our attention first on being an energy delivery company and then focus our actions on being the best energy delivery company," said Hafer.

At GPU Energy, the goal is to provide "unsurpassed customer service the first time, every time," said Michael Chesser, president and chief executive officer of GPU Energy. A team of GPU employees has developed a new vision that includes a "raving fans" philosophy in which everything the company does is organized around satisfying the customer. "Our customer focus will allow us to grow GPU Energy into a world-class service and delivery company," says Chesser.

In 2000, GPU Energy committed $56 million over three years for system reinforcements and upgrades. Since 1999, GPU Energy has been working to reduce by 40 percent the amount of time that customers are out of service.

Because residents and businesses have relied on GPU since it was founded in 1946, employees have always felt a strong link to their communities. "In our industry, we are an integral part of the community; the two are inseparable," says Chesser.

GPU is investing heavily in customer service and the reliability of its electric utility network. In Morris County, the company provides electric service to more than 160,000 customers in 39 communities.

Headquartered in Morristown, GPU provides utility and utility-related services to more than six million customers worldwide.

GPU's support for its communities includes contributions to youth and education, assisting those less fortunate, taking on issues like chemical dependency, and supporting cultural activities. For example, GPU works closely with America's Promise to help improve the health and well-being of at-risk children. Once a month, GPU employees serve healthy meals through Kids Café, the nation's largest charitable meal service program. The company also sponsors GPU Kids Count, a community awareness program about child hunger.

GPU financially supports Daytop-New Jersey, a special type of chemical dependency treatment center where adolescents gain control of their lives through professional help, and serves on its board of trustees. The company also offers a grants program in which employees or community members can obtain funding for such worthwhile community undertakings as special classroom projects. In addition, GPU distributes hundreds of computers and printers to non-profit organizations and schools. Teaming with the Princeton Center for Leadership Training, GPU's support has helped expand the New Jersey Peer-to-Peer initiative designed to prevent substance abuse.

Many of GPU's leaders are deeply involved in their communities. For example, Hafer has served on the U.S., New Jersey, and Pennsylvania chambers of commerce, as well as on various hospital boards. Chesser has served on the board of directors of the Child Welfare League of America, the Spokane Higher Education Council, and the Baltimore Chamber of Commerce.

As GPU's basic electric distribution business has deregulated, the company has taken several bold steps to enhance its performance by expanding in such non-regulated businesses as utility construction and telecommunications.

In 2000, GPU acquired MYR Group Inc., an infrastructure construction company that builds and maintains power lines for electric utilities, telecommunications companies, and industrial and commercial facilities. Operating through nine companies, MYR is the fifth largest electrical contractor and the eleventh largest specialty contractor in the U.S., with 1999 revenues of $477 million. During the five most recent years reported publicly, MYR achieved an annual growth rate of 41 percent in revenue and 28 percent in earnings per share.

In telecommunications, GPU's subsidiary, GPU Telcom, helped create America's Fiber Network (AFN), a company formed by six energy and telecommunications companies. The joint venture resulted in a 140,000-fiber-mile telecommunications network that connects major and secondary markets in the East and Midwest. The network helps businesses and homes in so-called second and third-tier markets to transmit and receive large amounts of information at high speed over the Internet.

Shortly after the creation of AFN, GPU Telcom entered into an agreement with Telergy Inc. to create Telergy Mid-Atlantic. This new venture markets broadband telecommunications services, such as voice, data, Internet, and video, to government facilities, educational institutions, and businesses. In a third venture, GPU Telcom formed a strategic partnership with Sting Communications, a broadband and wireless service provider based in Lebanon, Pennsylvania, to offer high-speed data services, including Internet and Intranet access in the Northeast.

Internationally, GPU delivers electricity to more than two million customers in the UK and Argentina through its subsidiaries Midlands Electricity plc and Emdersa. It serves another 1.4 million customers indirectly through its electric and gas transmission subsidiary, GasNet, PowerNet in Australia. GPU's other subsidiaries include GPU Advanced Resources Inc., GPU Nuclear Inc., and GPU Service Inc. □

Daily Record

For more than a century, the *Daily Record* has informed, entertained, and inspired residents of Morris County and surrounding communities.

Ernest Tomlinson published the first edition in 1900. Tomlinson believed that "a reliable presentation of the local news each day will be appreciated by the reading public, and the advertisers will be glad to have such a medium through which they can reach their patrons daily."

The newspaper thrived through three generations of Tomlinsons. In 1987, the Goodson Newspaper Group purchased the newspaper, and in 1998, Gannett Co. Inc., the nation's largest newspaper company, purchased the *Daily Record*.

Today, the *Daily Record* is among seven Gannett newspapers in New Jersey. The main office is located in Parsippany with bureaus in Dover and Morristown.

Ownership, locations, and the name of the newspaper have changed over the years, but the *Daily Record* has remained faithful to Tomlinson's original vision of providing local news and standing for the best interests of the community. As examples, in the 1960s, the newspaper joined in the crusade to establish the County College of Morris. Later, the *Daily Record* pushed for completion of two long-dormant highways, Route 24 and Interstate 287.

The *Daily Record* main office at 800 Jefferson Road in Parsippany. The *Daily Record* also has bureaus in Dover and Morristown.

The *Daily Record* is highly regarded for its coverage of high school sports in Morris County. In this award-winning photo, Randolph High School players react after a last-second field goal gives them the 1991 state championship over Montclair, in what many say was the most exciting high school football game in New Jersey history. Photo by Bob Karp/ *Daily Record*.

When abuses of the public pension system became rampant in the late 1980s, the *Daily Record* produced stories that led to system reform. When an epidemic of fatal heroin overdoses among young people plagued Morris County, the newspaper responded with an in-depth series examining the crisis and offering help to families.

The paper's staff of 300 includes a newsroom of 70 reporters, editors, and photographers who produce more than 22,000 local stories and thousands of color photographs each year. From the somber to the sublime, the *Daily Record* documents life in Morris County and portions of Sussex and Warren counties.

The newspaper has received numerous awards for its editorial and advertising content from community and professional groups, including the New Jersey Press Association and local Chamber of Commerce groups.

Additionally, the newspaper publishes the Shoppers Mart, Annual Forecast, and Living Guide, an annual supplement that is packed with information about Northwest New Jersey.

The *Daily Record's* presence in Morris County goes well beyond the printed page. As part of the Newspaper in Education program, the *Daily Record* provides 3,000 newspapers each day and other learning materials to local schools. The newspaper hosts an annual sports banquet to honor local athletes and coaches and to present scholarships. The Daily Record sponsors Operation Sunshine, a fund raising program that has sent thousands of Morris County children to summer camp.

The newspaper annually co-sponsors with the Morris County Chamber of Commerce a luncheon and awards program honoring small businesses, and is a co-sponsor of the annual Businesswoman of the Year award.

"No other medium can have the impact we have every day," said Walt Lafferty, president and publisher. "That's the beauty of a newspaper."

"The reason people read the *Daily Record* is because we give them the most comprehensive daily local news about their communities," said Lafferty. "Our commitment to Morris County is what separates us from other newspapers." □

Photo by L. A. Popp.

8

Technology, Manufacturing, and Distribution

Photo by L. A. Popp.

DPC Cirrus Inc.

In a former schoolroom in Chester, renowned scientist Arthur Babson fashioned a wooden model after an idea that had been spinning in his head for months. Babson was determined to find a more efficient way for clinical laboratories to conduct immunoassays, or tests that analyze and measure substances in minute concentrations within the body to help diagnose disease. At the time, test methods required a separation step to obtain accurate results from a blood sample. Existing separation methods were often conducted manually—a cumbersome process that was difficult to automate. The entire testing process could take days to complete.

IMMULITE 2000, a larger more automated version of IMMULITE, a high throughput analyzer, can process thousands of tests a day for higher volume laboratories.

"I knew that if I could automate the separation process, doctors would have test results within a couple of hours and could diagnose and treat disease much earlier," says Babson. Babson's idea worked, and on the strength of the patent he received for his idea, he eventually convinced investors to put up seed capital to start a company.

After forming Cirrus Diagnostics in 1987, Babson began hiring employees to help design his bench-top-sized brainchild, IMMULITE®. After four years of intensive effort, the Cirrus design team completed the IMMULITE system, including tests for thyroid and blood disorders, and began testing it in a few selected hospital laboratories. It was at this point that Diagnostic Products Corporation (DPC), the world's leading independent producer of immunodiagnostic products, initiated discussions with Cirrus and within a few short months completed the acquisition of the company. DPC renamed the company DPC Cirrus Inc. and moved what was now the instrumentation arm of DPC from the schoolhouse to the current location in Randolph. The acquisition of Cirrus by DPC was a perfect marriage of cultures and technologies. DPC had started as an entrepreneurial venture 20 years before and had become the premiere developer and marketer of blood test kits that could be put on the automated test system Cirrus had developed. Indeed today, the DPC IMMULITE systems offer a wider variety of tests than any other competitive system.

Six years later, DPC Cirrus, now as a part of DPC, completed the development of a larger, more automated version of IMMULITE, the IMMULITE 2000. DPC launched this system in March of 1998. The high throughput analyzer can process thousands of tests a day for higher volume laboratories.

"The first IMMULITE system was placed at Morristown Memorial Hospital," says Douglas Olson, President of DPC Cirrus. "Today, DPC's IMMULITE systems are used from doctors' offices to the largest medical centers in the world. DPC has sold more than 5,000 IMMULITE systems and more than 1,000 IMMULITE 2000 systems worldwide." The IMMULITE instrument enables lab technicians to test for allergy, anemia, diabetes, infectious disease, reproductive hormones, thyroid function, tumor markers, and more.

At the company's Morris County site, about 400 highly skilled people work on the systems from start to finish, including scientists, engineers, chemists, software developers, and technicians. "We make use of many different technologies to build these instruments, everything from optics to electronics to precision temperature controls. We work with vendors and suppliers to find the very best of these disparate pieces, and our experts pull them together to create the systems," explains James Guille, Director of Instrument Manufacturing.

In Service and Systems Support, technical specialists and trainers instruct customers on how to use the systems and also provide service and support to customers 24 hours a day, 7 days a week. "Our systems are state-of-the-art and simple to use," says Dotti Bernsten, Senior Director of Service and Systems Support. "They streamline the testing for diagnosing disease. What used to take days can now be done in an hour."

And what a difference a few hours can make in a life. "One of our most proud moments was when a doctor called up a lab with an urgent need for a thyroid stimulating hormone (TSH) test—a test that previously had taken a

When Art Babson first pitched the technology to investors at a Minneapolis restaurant, he had no idea that his invention would earn him the title of "New Jersey Inventor of the Year."

couple of days to get results. In a routine screen, an infant showed signs of hypothyroidism, which is a deficiency of thyroid secretion. If untreated, this deficiency can lead to deformity and mental disability," says Olson. "Because of IMMULITE, the doctor had the results in two hours. The infant was treated immediately for hypothyroidism and was spared a life of disability."

DPC Cirrus has many similar success stories, particularly in the area of in vitro fertilization. In the U.S., the DPC IMMULITE system is the technology used in labs to help analyze women's fertility cycles and enhance the possibility for fertilization. "I have two grandchildren because of this technology," says Carroll Simon-Scribner, Director of Human Resources. "I'm proud to be part of DPC Cirrus, and you will find that same pride within all of our employees. They come to work every day knowing that their ingenuity is changing lives."

As IMMULITE instrument and reagent sales continue to climb, currently making up 75 percent of DPC's worldwide business, DPC Cirrus once again finds itself bursting at the seams. To address the growth, in 2000 the company broke ground for a 90,000-square-foot building in Flanders that is expandable to 150,000 square feet. The new facility will include 36,000 square feet of manufacturing space, "enough to accommodate our existing product lines and our products of the future," says Guille.

"And the future is what it's all about. Our Engineering, Chemistry, and Software Teams are now leading the organization forward with multiple cutting-edge products in various stages of development. We've been able to attract and retain highly competent and energized staff members who are the foundation of our success," says Olson.

Babson's rugged wooden model has long been replaced by high-powered machinery with impressive potential. When he first pitched the technology to investors at a Minneapolis restaurant, he had no idea that his invention would earn him the title of "New Jersey Inventor of the Year" and give birth to a multi-million dollar business. He says, "At the end of the day, our technology provides better health care. We enable doctors to measure things, in infinitesimally small quantities, which helps them make better decisions about treatment." □

In 2000 DPC Cirrus broke ground for a 90,000-square-foot building in Flanders that is expandable to 150,000 square feet.

At the company's Morris County site, about 400 highly skilled people work on the systems from start to finish, including scientists, engineers, chemists, software developers, and technicians. Pictured is the Instrument Manufacturing team.

BASF Corporation

The yellow paint on a school bus, the fibers in a carpet, prescription medicine in a cabinet, the polymers in yogurt containers—all seemingly different products with a common foundation, they are among the thousands of quality products offered by BASF Corporation, a leading manufacturer and marketer of chemicals and related materials.

Based in Mount Olive at the International Trade Center, BASF Corporation is the North American affiliate of BASF Group, which has its global headquarters in Ludwigshafen, Germany, and is one of the world's leading chemical companies. BASF Corporation employs approximately 16,000 people in North America at some 50 locations.

BASF Corporate Headquarters in Mount Olive, New Jersey.

"We don't make a lot of the products you buy. We make a lot of the products you buy better.®" is the corporate theme that underscores the enormous scope of applications of BASF products, as well as the company's commitment to quality, service, and diversity.

BASF's operations in North America rest on two strong pillars. One is its chemicals and chemical-related business, including basic, intermediate, and specialty chemicals, polymers, fibers, dispersions, and automotive and industrial coatings. These account for about two-thirds of the company's overall sales. The second pillar is the company's increasingly robust business in Health and Nutrition, which comprises pharmaceuticals, agricultural products, nutritional products, and pharmaceutical chemicals.

All business units—Chemicals, Coatings and Colorants, Polymers, Fiber Products, Agricultural Products, and Pharmaceuticals—are represented in Mount Olive. In total, the BASF site there has more than 2,700 full-time employees and contractors who work in operating business groups and administrative functions. In addition, BASF operates manufacturing facilities in New Jersey. These are located in Whippany, Belvidere, South Brunswick, and Washington.

"New Jersey is a good platform from which we can accomplish our objectives," says Peter Oakley, Chairman and Chief Executive Officer. "The Garden State offers a progressive, creative, and internationally-minded environment, which enables us to not only master demanding challenges facing the chemical industry, but seize new opportunities."

BASF Corporation moved into its then newly-built North American headquarters in 1994. Previously, headquarters' employees were housed in various locations in Morris County. The move to the warm, rose-colored brick facility nestled in 150 wooded acres in Mount Olive brought them together and helped strengthen the organization's corporate culture.

Shortly afterwards, the New Jersey Business and Industry Association awarded BASF its Good Neighbor Award for contributing to the economic health of New Jersey.

Today, BASF is continuing to help boost the local economy, as well as community life through corporate donations and employee volunteer activities. With a primary focus on enhancing science education, BASF has created and nurtured partnerships with local schools by providing, for example, technology grants, science education workshops, and applied learning programs, such as a robotics competition. BASF also serves as host to the Morris County Chamber of Commerce Business and Education Together program, pairing local high school students with business leaders.

In addition, BASF employees organize blood drives for the American Red Cross and sponsor fundraising events for organizations such as the United Way of Morris County, the American Cancer Society, and the American Heart Association. The BASF African-American Employees Group founded and hosts the annual Al Chisholm Golf Tournament, benefiting the scholarship program of the United Negro College Fund.

BASF's impact is also felt well beyond Morris County and the Garden State. In North America as a whole, the company ranks among the top competitors in its markets.

The polystyrene production facility in South Brunswick, New Jersey.

"We are highly committed to North America as a very demanding but also rewarding growth market, and we are continuously strengthening our position in all relevant areas, from research and development to manufacturing and marketing," says Oakley.

BASF's largest North American production facilities are located in Freeport, Texas; Geismar, Louisiana; Wyandotte, Michigan; Anderson, South Carolina; and Altamira, Mexico. Major research centers are located in Worcester, Massachusetts; Research Triangle Park and Charlotte, North Carolina; and Southfield and Wyandotte, Michigan.

At all of its North American facilities, BASF meets or exceeds the environmental health and safety requirements of the communities in which it operates. A specific facet of this commitment is evident in Mount Olive, where the company is using only 40 of its 150 acres in order to preserve the surrounding natural woodland. Within this scenic environment are walking trails, tall hardwoods and softwoods, wildflowers, and grasses for local wildlife.

From a business point of view, BASF is positioned as a return-focused company that generates long-term growth and strong profitability from its operations, as is reflected in its ongoing capital investments. Through 2002, BASF's capital investment program will direct about $800 million a year into new plants and equipment. These investments in worldscale operations span the scope of BASF operations in North America.

The new acetylene facility at BASF's manufacturing site in Geismar, Louisiana.

Ongoing capital investments, technical and operating prowess, targeted acquisitions, and a continually strengthened customer focus are advancing BASF's growing market presence. By 1999, the company's sales in North America have grown by nearly one-third, income from operations has more than tripled, and cash flow has more than doubled. Similarly sales per employee have doubled, productivity has steadily improved, production costs have stabilized or decreased, and product quality and customer service have been enhanced.

Bring Your Child to Work Day is an annual event at BASF.

In the years ahead, BASF expects to add dozens of innovative new products and leading-edge technologies. The company is repeatedly being recognized for its efficient, quality, and customer-focused businesses—clear results of a long-standing, integrated approach toward its business. The company is especially known for making the most of its integrated approach to manufacturing, research and, indeed, its overall management philosophy. This philosophy, together with the maximum integration of infrastructure, process, energy, and waste management, is known as Verbund, a German word meaning "linked" or "integrated" to the maximum degree.

What began as a research breakthrough in dyestuffs more than 130 years ago at Badische Anilin & Soda-Fabrik (hence BASF), has evolved into one of the world's largest chemical companies with a total workforce of approximately 105,000 employees. BASF maintains business relationships in scores of countries and operates production facilities in about 40. These are supported by a unique portfolio of products—one that will continue to meet the needs of customers and consumers better in Morris County, North America, and around the world. □

RFL Electronics Inc.

When a blackout sent a ripple of chaos across New York City in 1965, engineers at RFL Electronics Inc. in Boonton Township saw an opportunity. At the time, the power industry had unsophisticated ways of protecting transmission grids. "A tree would fall on a power line or a bolt of lightning would strike a pole, and a domino effect could occur, knocking out power from substation to substation," says Steven Gilliatt, president of RFL Electronics Inc. The blackout sparked new communications ideas and, ultimately, helped the company evolve as a leading supplier of communications and protection products and services that assist the power industry in protecting transmission grids.

The RFL team located within the Boonton Township facility is made up of about 175 people, including highly skilled engineers, test and service technicians, assemblers who work in manufacturing, administrative staff members, and a core sales team.

RFL's solutions for the power industry are among dozens of innovative developments that date back to the company's founding by Richard W. Seabury in 1922. Originally known as Radio Frequency Laboratories, early work at the company centered on research and development, including the development of amplifier circuits, a single-control broadcast receiver, and an automatic volume control.

Over the years, the business has taken several remarkable paths. In the late 1920s, RFL was producing receivers and transmitters for aircraft. In 1929, war hero General James H. Doolittle was the first aviator to successfully demonstrate a "blind" flight with instrument-only take off and landing using an RFL radio. Signs of the old airstrip remain near the property, but it is used today as a community soccer field.

During World War II, RFL was active in the design and manufacture of electrical test and calibration instrumentation and magnet charging and de-magnetizing equipment. Numerous innovations followed, from thermocontrol and measurement instruments for industrial applications to toroidal coils used in filter applications. As the company introduced new products, spin-off companies emerged, including several successful companies that operate in Morris County today. Along the way, the company's name and ownership changed several times, as did its operating units and branches, reflecting its ability to recalibrate according to market needs.

"Historically, the RFL team has been known for their inventive nature and for their ability to transform our business based on industry needs," says Gilliatt.

By the 1980s, RFL was deeply engrained in the development and manufacture of instrumentation and communications products and systems. The company introduced the first substation-hardened multiplexer systems to the electric utility industry and has since released second and third generation products. In 2000, RFL introduced the first redundant capability into the multiplexer offerings, which provides continuous component backup so there is no service interruption for the customer.

Today, RFL is a wholly owned subsidiary of SL Industries, a publicly traded holding company, and provides a wide range of communications and protective relaying products, application support, and customized systems to a variety of industries. The company supplies products to investor-owned electric utilities and municipalities across the country and around the world. In addition, RFL provides products and services to railroad and highway industries, government agencies, and engineering consulting firms. Much of the New Jersey turnpike utilizes RFL communications control equipment for traffic signaling.

RFL's 88,000-square-foot facility located within 17 lush acres in the Rockaway Valley of Boonton Township, provides a wide range of communications and protective relaying products, application support, and customized systems to a variety of industries.

RFL also offers a complete range of technical services, including project specifications, system design, project management, commissioning, and training.

Although much has changed at RFL since 1922, Morris County continues to be an ideal home base for the company. The 88,000-square-foot facility is located within 17 lush acres in the Rockaway Valley of Boonton Township and includes 50,000 square feet of manufacturing space. Inside these walls, products are designed, developed, and deployed in a highly automated environment. What begins on the manufacturing floor with small components culminates in the final production of large cabinets for power protection and transportation controls.

About 175 people make up the RFL team, including highly skilled engineers, test and service technicians, and assemblers who work in manufacturing. The engineering team designs and develops all RFL products. Administrative staff members are also located within the Boonton Township facility. A core sales team operates out of Boonton Township, along with regional offices throughout the U.S. and abroad. RFL has expanded its presence worldwide through technical sales support with offices covering North America, Europe, Latin America, and Asia Pacific. In addition, RFL has an extensive network of representatives and distributors worldwide.

RFL's products provide valuable services to consumers and businesses. "Because of the Internet, the demand for power reliability and capacity has increased tremendously. When you lose power, it can be devastating," says Gilliatt. "In any given year, U.S. businesses lose billions due to power outages. We offer products and services that help utility companies provide reliable power to their customers."

RFL's products are helping national and regional highway systems as they meet the growing demand for travel. Inadequate capacity, poor connections, increased highway usage, and weather pose challenges that are disruptive to highways. RFL products help monitor and provide surveillance of busy highway systems.

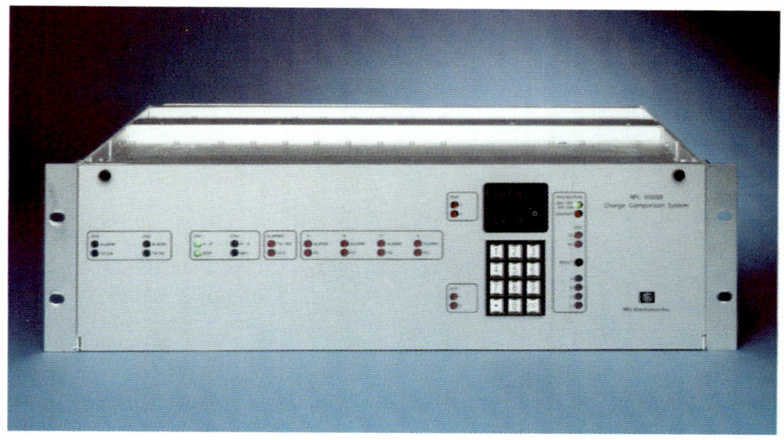

For nearly 80 years, RFL has provided quality products and services to its customers worldwide.

Products offered by RFL include multiplexers, powerline carrier systems, control and telemetry technology, teleprotection systems, relaying systems, and video and digital communications systems.

Each of RFL's products is designed and manufactured according to the highest standards. "Our commitment to quality means that our products meet our customers' specifications, standards of performance and reliability, as well as on-time delivery," says Gilliatt. RFL is ISO 9001 registered by an independent, internationally recognized certification body. RFL's quality management system ensures that all products and service-related processes are documented and audited regularly.

"We are proud of this company because of its history and longevity and the ability of our people to perform at a high level," says Gilliatt. □

Lieutenant Jimmy Doolittle, aviation pioneer and war hero, with his Consolidated NY-2 is pictured on the Radio Frequency Laboratories, Inc., Aircraft Radio Corporation Division, Airdrome in Rockaway Valley, Boonton Township, New Jersey, in 1929.

ASCO

ASCO worldwide headquarters, Florham Park, New Jersey.

Founded in 1888 in New York City, ASCO (Automatic Switch Company) initially developed and manufactured switching controls for elevators. The company's innovative thinkers soon applied this technology to other ventures, and ASCO branched into two distinct businesses, ASCO Power Technologies and ASCO Valve, Inc, both headquartered in Florham Park. These businesses, now members of the Emerson Electric family, are world leaders in their respective fields of Power Distribution & Control and Fluid Control.

Since the beginning ASCO has been constantly striving to anticipate and satisfy customer needs and provide technological solutions to challenging control problems. In 1910 it introduced the first solenoid valve for controlling the flow of process liquids and gases. It will remain at the forefront of its fields, with new innovations like Site Web VPI, introduced in 2000, a Windows™-based power monitoring system that allows multiple engine generators to be controlled from the Internet. ASCO will never cease its quest for cutting-edge products and services.

ASCO Power Technologies

Nearly every system within a business or home depends on electric power. When that power fails, it can not only be disruptive, but in some cases—disastrous.

"Our products help keep your power on," says Armand Visioli, president of ASCO Power Technologies. "We don't generate the power, but we control, distribute, transfer, monitor, measure, manage, display, maintain, service, and communicate with it."

ASCO Power Technologies is the world's leading manufacturer of automatic transfer switches, power control systems, and industrial control products. It also operates a 24-hour international service organization, ASCO Services Inc., to support its customers worldwide.

"In the past 100 years, we have pioneered every major innovation in power transfer technology," says Mr. Visioli. "Today, we move about 100 million kilowatts of power a day."

Around the world, ASCO Power Technologies has installed more than 500,000 automatic transfer switches. "Because we have highly reliable products, our technology can be found in the majority of American hospitals, in some of the world's largest financial data centers, such as New York City, in virtually every FAA control and radar site, and on almost every U.S. Navy vessel and those of member NATO countries. These are critical emergency power applications," says Mr. Visioli.

When power fails, ASCO's technology immediately senses the loss of utility power, signals the generator to start and restore power, and moves the vital loads of power from one source to the other, preventing any disasters and inconveniences that can occur when power is disrupted.

ASCO's products are increasingly finding their way into homes. "When you buy a backup or "stand-by" generator for your home, the National Electric Code mandates that you use approved transfer switches between power sources," says Mr. Visioli. "Our controls and switches help ensure that power is transferred seamlessly. For example, when a storm knocks out utility, you do not need to worry about your sump pump stopping, freezing pipes, or food spoiling in your refrigerator."

At the Florham Park facility, plus a 140,000-square-foot manufacturing and engineering site in Parsippany, ASCO Power Technologies is home to over 600 employees. It is one of the largest non-pharmaceutical manufacturers in Morris County. There are also design and manufacturing facilities in Brantford, Canada, Stockton, California, and Lerma, Mexico, and sales and service offices around the globe.

Consistent with its charter, ASCO Power Technologies is today actively formulating technological solutions to meet the demand for products and services created by the deregulation of the Electrical Utility Industry and the emerging distributed generation market.

"Our worldwide leadership is possible because of the dedication and expertise of ASCO employees," says Mr. Visioli. "They possess the high-tech skills needed to build complex products, and they follow rigorous standards to ensure quality. Our employees understand that quality is not bolted on; it's built in."

ASCO Valve, Inc.

Sharing corporate headquarters with ASCO Power Technologies is ASCO Valve, Inc., a world leader in fluid control technology and the inventor of the world's first solenoid valve.

"Wherever there is a need to control the flow of water, oil, gas, or air, you will usually find an ASCO product," says Paul Petrignani, vice president, marketing. "You probably cannot go through a day without being impacted by one of our valves."

In Florham Park, ASCO Valve is home to about 670 employees who work in manufacturing, research, design and engineering groups, testing labs, a pilot plant, in-house support services, sales, and marketing. Worldwide, ASCO Valve has manufacturing facilities, sales offices, and distributors in more than 40 countries.

The company offers 2,000 standard valves and more than 30,000 specialized valves in a variety of shapes, sizes, and capabilities, depending upon the fluid control required. For instance, while a doctor uses one of ASCO's micro-miniature solenoid valves to keep saline flowing to a patient's eye during microsurgery, some of the world's largest refineries are using ASCO Valve technology to regulate and control the flow of oil and gas.

Product lines include ASCO Red-Hat, which offers 2-, 3-, and 4-way solenoid valves for the most demanding fluid control applications; ASCO General Controls, which are designed to regulate the flow of fuel gas, liquid propane, and all grades of fuel in commercial and industrial applications; ASCO Scientific, which offers micro-miniature precision valves used in critical applications, such as in the medical/analytical field; and ASCO Pneumatic that provides 3- and 4-way directional control valves, filters, regulators, and lubricators.

Every valve goes through a rigorous development process that begins in the product design and development group, progresses through the industry's first computer integrated engineering center, advances through high-tech assembly and testing laboratories, and culminates with production in the on-site pilot plant.

"Our quality products can be found in numerous industrial applications and applications that impact consumers," says Petrignani. As examples, ASCO's innovative technology can be found in nuclear power plants, pulp and paper mills, and pharmaceutical manufacturing facilities. Consumers will find ASCO valves in ice machines, hotel industrial washing and drying machines, and at the pub on brewing machines.

ASCO valves also show up in the entertainment world, inside the mechanical shark in *Jaws* and in special effects equipment found on floats in the Macy's Thanksgiving Day Parade and at Disney World.

"We have a history of developing innovative solutions for our customers," says Petrignani. "It's our legacy, and it is the foundation that will fuel our growth in the 21st century." □

ASCO's automatic transfer switch being adjusted during final assembly.

The ASCO Valve Laboratory handles the initial assembly of prototypes and conducts rigorous performance testing.

MAERSK INC.

From toys to textiles, from perishable fruits to footwear, from wearing apparel to electronic goods, Maersk Sealand ensures that imported and exported goods arrive safely and quickly to their destinations worldwide. Few people in the United States realize that 95 percent of foreign trade moves by ship.

Nestled in the beautiful business campus of Giralda Farms in Madison, New Jersey, is located the North American headquarters of one of the world's leading containership lines serving world trade.

A container is loaded onto a truck.

Established in 1943, Maersk Inc. represents the North American agency network for Maersk Sealand. Today, Maersk Inc. operates 100 agency or container shipping-related offices in North America with a staff of 3,000, serving the United States, Canada, Central America, and the Caribbean. The ocean carrier's North American headquarters in Madison, New Jersey, are home to 400 employees. In 1988, the company relocated to Madison from the World Trade Center in New York City.

With a network of 325 offices in 100 countries, 10,000 employees, and 250 vessels, Maersk Sealand is the largest containership line in the world; the largest U.S. flag operator in the world; and the third largest operator of container terminals in the world.

Maersk Sealand is the container shipping division of the A.P. Moller Group of Copenhagen, Denmark. The A.P. Moller Group, with world headquarters in Copenhagen, Denmark, has more than 50,000 employees in 100 countries around the world. Originally a steamship company, the group now runs a diverse portfolio of successful businesses around the world. Founded in 1904 with the purchase of a second-hand steamer by Arnold Peter Moller, the company has grown into a fleet of more than 250 vessels, tankers, bulk and special vessels, supply ships, and drilling rigs. In addition to shipping, the A.P. Moller Group is engaged in exploration for and production of oil and gas, shipbuilding, industry, air transport, IT services, and retailing.

Unique features of the A.P. Moller Group include a private shipbuilding yard called Odense Steel Shipyard, which has produced some of the largest, most technologically-advanced 6,600 TEU containerships in the world; Maersk Container Industry—a private manufacturing facility for building dry and refrigerated containers, supplying a fleet that now numbers over 1,200,000 containers; a global supply chain management company called Maersk Logistics; and an information technology company called Maersk Data.

In 1998, Maersk Sealand introduced the largest containership to call the U.S. East Coast—at 1,043 feet and equal in length to 3 1/2 football fields—*REGINA MAERSK* made her maiden voyage into New York Harbor with a flotilla of watercraft following her as she paused for a ceremonial salute to New York City and then later docked at Port Newark, New Jersey, to load and discharge cargo.

"The superships of the future are here today, and they are reshaping the container trade," stated Tommy Thomsen, president & CEO of Maersk Inc. in Madison, New Jersey. The ship features a 74,600-horsepower engine driving a 30-foot, 6-bladed propeller 94 revolutions a minute for a cruising speed of 25 knots—about 29 MPH. She also carries four auxiliary engines, generating more than 12,000 kilowatts—enough to supply approximately 6,000 homes in the state of New Jersey per month with light. A centralized computer links 2,800 sensors in the engine room and cargo holds to ensure safe operation and cargo handling.

In 1999, the company introduced a similar vessel—10 percent larger—to the trade. Along with super ships, Maersk Sealand is also known for its super ports. Because of the huge consumer market in North America, the company operates some of the busiest ports of call in the world. In total, Maersk Inc. operates 14 terminals in North America. "With the growth of world trade—ports become vital engines for growth. In Port Elizabeth, New Jersey, we are constructing an expanded 350-acre facility; in Los Angeles,

***SUSAN MAERSK*—one of the largest container ships in the world.**

Right: The Maersk Inc. headquarters in Madison, New Jersey. Below: A container truck in Hong Kong.

construction of our future 485-acre container terminal progresses on schedule for its opening in July 2002—considered the largest proprietary container terminal in the world and equal in size to 366 football fields. These are key indicators of the importance we place on ports and their value in strong supply chains," stated Thomsen.

"With both projects, we are launching a new era in the evolution of ports in one of the most important trade centers of the world. We want our customers to be able to compete in world markets in a stronger, more effective way and are designing our services around this simple goal. Equally important, companies are made of people—and talent is the key in today's competitive marketplace. Those companies that offer employees an environment to learn and grow will advance faster than others," according to Thomsen.

"At Maersk Sealand, we are excited about the opportunities ahead of us. Customers have a choice—and our focus is on being the best choice for our customers. We're building and investing in a portfolio of services to create a company unlike any other," stated Thomsen.

For Maersk Inc., a tightly knit network of subsidiaries and branch offices ensures that every step of every process follows the highest company and industry standards. U.S. subsidiaries include Maersk Line, Limited, which is a U.S. flag operation in Norfolk, Virginia, that serves the U.S. military and the government; a trucking company in Richmond, Virginia, that manages the ground transport of goods; Maersk Logistics, a supply chain management company in Madison, New Jersey; and Maersk Data, an information technology company in Morristown, New Jersey. ☐

Honeywell International

You come in contact with products Honeywell makes or helps its customers make every day. Honeywell makes air travel safer and more efficient, your home or office more comfortable, your car run better, safer, longer. The company even helps the space shuttle perform better.

Honeywell's Global Headquarters, Morristown.

Honeywell is a $24-billion advanced-technology and manufacturing company that provides a variety of materials, products, and integrated solutions for customers worldwide.

The company employs about 120,000 people in nearly 100 countries, including approximately 1,600 employees at its global headquarters in Morristown. It is traded on the New York Stock Exchange under the symbol HON, and it is also traded on the London and Pacific exchanges. Honeywell is one of the 30 companies that make up the Dow Jones Industrial Average, and it is a component of the Standard & Poor 500 index.

Honeywell serves four business segments: Aerospace Solutions; Automation and Control; Performance Materials; and Power and Transportation Products.

Aerospace Solutions - In the aerospace industry, Honeywell is a leading supplier of integrated avionics solutions, including flight management, flight safety, and cockpit display technologies; space navigation systems; aircraft engines; landing gear systems; and airport lighting and monitoring systems. The company prides itself on being the leading provider of nose-to-tail and gate-to-gate coverage to the aircraft industry through its products, services, and integrated solutions. The company's products or services are on or support nearly every class of aircraft flying today.

Honeywell is also leading the airline industry in the evolution to a more efficient air traffic control system, which will open up the skies beyond traditional air routes to make air travel more efficient, faster, and less costly. Its space business supports the Space Shuttle, International Space Station, and most satellite and space exploration programs. Honeywell technology has been on board every manned U.S. space flight since the Mercury era.

Automation and Control - Honeywell is a leader in offering integrated automation and control systems and products, which provide comfort, security, and energy efficiency to homes and commercial buildings. Its industrial control solutions enable manufacturing facilities to operate more safely efficiently. The company is in the vanguard of developing Internet- and wireless-based systems that integrate its comfort, security, and fire protection systems.

Performance Materials - Honeywell provides specialty chemicals, plastics, fibers, electronic materials, and specialty waxes for many industries and applications. For example, it is the leading developer of CFC-free refrigerants used in commercial and residential refrigeration and air-conditioning applications. Its polymer fibers are found in a host of applications, ranging from carpeting and seatbelts to bullet-proof material used in law enforcement.

Power and Transportation Products - Honeywell manufactures such well-known consumer brands as Prestone® antifreeze/coolant; Fram® oil, air, transmission, and fuel filters; Bendix® brakes; Garrett® turbochargers; and Autolite® spark plugs. The company also offers the innovative Parallon® 75 turbogenerator, a compact, self-contained unit that uses a microturbine to convert natural gas and other fuels into electricity for on-site power generation. The turbogenerator can be used as an alternative energy supply for stadiums, hotels, convention centers, and restaurants.

Most recently, Honeywell has embraced the Internet. The company leads its industry peers in the transformation from the old economy to the new. It has launched three global Internet e-hubs—MyPlant.com, MyFacilities.com, and MyAircraft.com (joint venture with United Technologies and i2 Technologies)—to reach customers and help them solve operational problems. It also has applied Web-enabled technology through its business processes to make them more efficient and more customer focused.

Honeywell is the world's leading supplier of comfort and automation solutions for homes and commercial buildings and is developing Web-enabled systems that help homeowners control their home environment.

"Honeywell has a long heritage of innovation and achievement," says Alan Painter, director of community affairs. "We attribute a large part of our ongoing success to our commitment to employee learning. Every employee is required to participate in at least 40 hours of educational programs each year." At the Morristown facility, Honeywell offers a comprehensive learning curriculum and learning centers to help employees in their professional development.

In addition to a commitment to learning, Honeywell employees believe in good corporate citizenship. In a given year, according to Painter, Honeywell's financial contributions to education, the arts, and civic organizations total more than $20 million. Additionally, employees at world headquarters in Morristown donate their time through Honeywell's volunteerism program, which includes employee participation in Habitat for Humanity projects, fundraisers to support scholarships for inner city children, a community soup kitchen, and projects that support United Way agencies. □

Smiths Industries Actuation Systems, Inc.

With 95 commercial airlines, the U.S. government, and international companies like Boeing and Lockheed Martin as key customers, industry analysts might say the sky's the limit for Smiths Industries Actuation Systems.

Technically speaking, the company is in "the sub-system integration of high specification motion controls for the aerospace and defense industries," says Dave Sapio, president. In other words, Smiths Industries Actuation Systems provides the technology that controls many of the vital functions found on aircraft and military land vehicles, such as actuators that cause wing flaps to move or trigger the launch of munitions.

Sapio explains that the company designs, manufactures, and maintains control technologies in three markets: aircraft controls, both fixed and rotary for commercial and military industries; land vehicle controls, including turret and launch controls; and controls for smart munitions, such as fin guidance positioning.

In recent years, the company has perfected the development of these controls so that they act in an integrated way, helping pilots and drivers to better manage the range of utilities on board, from electrical power generation to environmental controls.

Smiths Industries Actuation Systems provides the technology that controls many of the vital functions found on aircraft and military land vehicles.

"Our aim is to become the world's leading designer and manufacturer of electromechanical motion control systems in our selected markets," says Sapio. He adds that the company's most recent alliance is propelling the company in that very direction. In 2000, the company was acquired by Smiths Industries, an international company with 16,000 employees working in 50 worldwide businesses. Smith Industries operates in three business areas: aerospace systems and equipment, which now includes the Whippany-based Smiths Industries Actuation Systems; specialized industrial products, such as air movement and cable protection systems; and medical systems, which includes the manufacture and distribution of disposable medical devices.

"By joining Smiths Industries, we are part of a major corporation with an established, global presence in the same aerospace and defense markets that we serve," says Sapio. "The dynamic combination of their products with ours is creating a very strong offering for customers."

Smiths Industries Actuation Systems' history dates back to the late '40s, when Airborne Accessories and General Brass merged to create a components-manufacturing operation for military and commercial aircraft. In 1989, the company moved from its Hillside location to its current home in Whippany. The facility houses about 290 employees and includes 117,000 square feet of office and manufacturing space. "We design and manufacture all of our components at the Whippany site and purchase 50 percent of our materials from companies within the area," says Sapio.

In 1989, the company moved from its Hillside location to its current home in Whippany. The facility houses about 290 employees and includes 117,000 square feet of office and manufacturing space.

Along with administrative support, employees at the Whippany facility include systems engineers, mechanical designers, electrical designers, assemblers, and test technicians.

"Our employees are the fuel that keeps us moving in the right direction," says Sapio. "We are immersed in an industry where there is pressure to perform at higher levels within declining budgets. Our employees understand the magnitude of this challenge, take ownership of it, and work shoulder-to-shoulder with management to solve problems." □

9

EDUCATION

Photo by Joel Sartore.

County College of Morris

From the tiny cells in the human body to the expansive wonders of the universe, the County College of Morris offers a diverse range of classes to help learners achieve their professional and personal goals.

Additionally, the college is consistently responsive to the needs of the regional business community by offering education and training programs that address occupational demands, as well as individual development.

The beautiful County College of Morris campus blossoms with many flowering trees each spring.

The two-year community college, located on 218 acres in Randolph, provides quality education for full- and part-time students. The college awards more associate's degrees than any community college in New Jersey, features the largest music department among community colleges in the state, and grants more associate's degrees for registered nurses than any public or private school in New Jersey.

"About 72 percent of our students transfer to four-year institutions, which gives us one of the highest transfer rates to four-year colleges among community colleges in New Jersey," said Dr. Edward Yaw, president. "Our list reads like a who's who: We have students transferring to Yale, Cornell, the University of Pennsylvania, and many other outstanding universities."

Many students also stay close to home, giving local businesses access to a qualified pool of potential employees. Businesses can post their job openings, free of charge, at strategic sites on campus and on the college Web site. They can utilize the college's Career Services & Cooperative Education program to recruit interns and co-ops. Through the program, the college links students in 24 different majors to career opportunities by placing them in jobs that give them work-related experience and academic credit toward graduation, as well as paving the way for possible future employment within the county. Because hundreds of graduates are now working in local companies, the college has established five corporate alumni clubs within Morris County.

In addition to providing potential employees, the college offers businesses a variety of learning opportunities. Through the College-in-the-Company program, employees can take college-credit courses while at their job sites before or after work, during their lunch hours, or on weekends. Through the Center for Business & Technology, employees have access to customized training programs developed by the college to meet specific company needs, such as the course on medical terminology recently offered to employees of a local pharmaceutical company.

Addressing the educational needs of the community has been the college's mission since 1968, when the County College of Morris officially opened its doors in a single building, Henderson Hall, serving about 600 full-time and 700 part-time students. As the community's educational requirements expanded over the next three decades, so did the college. To guarantee that students would always have access to the latest equipment and facilities, the college established a proactive technology strategy and constructed a high-technology building. The library was expanded to include television and audio production studios. A child-care center opened. Science labs were updated. A six-lane swimming facility was added to the health and physical education building.

Along with facilities and equipment, new courses are continually added, such as classes in veterinary technology, radiography, process technology for manufacturing, pharmacy technology, and early childhood education. Internet courses are available, as well as television classes on the local cable channel.

A Medical Laboratory Technology student draws a chemical solution from a tube.

To date, about 30,000 students have graduated from the County College of Morris. Each year, about 8,000 full- and part-time students benefit from the 70 different degrees and certificate programs. Students earn credit toward associate's degrees in arts, science, applied science, or certificates. Annually, 8,500 adult learners take non-credit courses. Classes are offered at the main campus, at Headquarters Plaza in Morristown, and at several local high schools.

"If you peek into our classrooms, one of the first things you notice is the diversity," said Dr. Joseph Nazzaro, executive director, college advancement and planning. "As examples, we have a 13-year-old honors student accelerating through our physics program, and we recently graduated a woman in her 70s. She told me that going back to college to complete her degree was one of the greatest experiences of her life."

Different ability levels and cultural and ethnic backgrounds are also evident at the college. "Every individual is unique with different capabilities and goals," said Nazzaro.

About 80 percent of students are from Morris County and surrounding counties. There are also students from more than 50 foreign countries, enriching the ethnic and cultural blend at the college.

County College of Morris President Edward J. Yaw speaks with students.

County College of Morris campus bursts with fall colors.

Although students' educational goals differ, they choose the County College of Morris for the same reasons. "The college is known for its exceptional faculty, state-of-the-art facilities and technology, and a wide range of educational programs," said Yaw. "The college is also known for its value. We offer high quality education at an affordable cost. Plus, students benefit from the expertise and experience of adjunct faculty brought in from nearby Fortune 500 companies."

For those with a competitive spirit, the college boasts a top-ranking athletic program, capturing 35 New Jersey Garden State Athletic Conference team championships and 30 Region XIX championships, and participating in 31 national tournaments. Intercollegiate athletic programs thrive at the college, including baseball, basketball, golf, ice hockey, and soccer for men, and basketball, golf, and softball for women. Intramural sports feature everything from bowling to volleyball to flag football.

Not only do the diverse classes and programs enhance students' lives, but they also support the community at large. More than 50,000 people a year visit the campus to enjoy the planetarium, attend sporting events, foreign film series, fine arts programs, and lectures. High school swim teams use the aquatics center for practice and competitions.

Through the college's Partnership for Quality Education, speakers provide lectures, presentations, and demonstrations tailored for children, families, adults, and senior citizens at local community sites.

As college leaders have done since 1968, Nazzaro said the college will continue to identify the educational needs of students, businesspeople, and residents and build programs to address those needs. "Our intention is to offer courses to anyone, anywhere. The doors to education are open at the County College of Morris." □

College of Saint Elizabeth

In the late 1800s, higher education for women was almost unheard of in New Jersey, until a group of women—the Sisters of Charity—set out to change history forever.

Marching forward with a bold mission and an undaunted spirit, the Sisters of Charity established the College of Saint Elizabeth in 1899, the first four-year Catholic college for women in New Jersey and the only college in New Jersey to award baccalaureate degrees to women.

"For more than a century, the College of Saint Elizabeth has encouraged women to pursue challenging ideas, explore their place in the world, and meet exceptional women who have blazed the trails before them," said Sister Francis Raftery, president.

What began with a core of six students has blossomed into a lively campus cradled within the rolling hills of historic Morristown. Today, more than 1,800 students from 26 countries benefit from the programs offered at the college, including the liberal arts college for women, coeducational undergraduate programs for adults, and coeducational graduate programs. The college offers 28 baccalaureate degrees, seven master's degrees, and preparation for ministry through the Center for Theological and Spiritual Development.

"Students come to the College of Saint Elizabeth to be part of an ethical, spiritual learning community, where they are guaranteed sustenance inside and outside the classroom," said Dr. Johanna Glazewski, vice president and dean for academic affairs. The small class sizes foster insightful thinking, ethical analysis, engaging dialogue, and enduring friendships.

The college's location is a magnet for students who treasure the calm, historic campus, but also delight in the flurry of culture surrounding the Morristown area. Photo by Stephen Spartana.

The more than 100-year-old College of Saint Elizabeth, Morris County's first women's college, offers today's women a well-rounded liberal arts education. Students enjoy challenging academic work, spiritual and social training, as well as vibrant athletic programs. Photo by Chris Faytok.

Academic opportunities at the college are intellectual, diverse, and centered on ethical/social responsibility, all reflective of the foundation of values established by the Sisters of Charity. As examples, at the Holocaust Education Resource Center, students grapple with ideas on how to prevent human rights atrocities. In the Food and Nutrition Department, students apply science to do everything from developing high-tech cooking appliances to menus for hospital patients. In the Justice Studies program, police officers and lawyers learn how to better serve minorities, women, and children.

The college's location is another magnet for students, who treasure the calm, historic campus, but also delight in the flurry of culture surrounding the Morristown area. From telecommunications to health care, the location gives students access to the corporate community and institutions where they can cultivate job experience and demonstrate their compassion for the community.

The size and scope of the college have changed, but its mission to be a community of learning and leadership remains steadfast. To further that vision, the college is undergoing a 15-year, $63-million renovation and construction program that will result in a new center for fine and performing arts, additional classrooms, and a vibrant renewal of many of the college's landmark buildings.

"My greatest hope is that we will remain faithful to the mission of the college—that we will prepare leaders who not only have their own dreams, but also have a dream that will impact this global society in which we live," said Sister Francis Raftery. □

Fairleigh Dickinson University

For more than a half-century, Fairleigh Dickinson University has played a pivotal role in educating the leaders of New Jersey and the nation. One of the largest independent nonsectarian institutions of higher education in the state, FDU serves approximately 9,000 students, and more than 90,000 alumni live and work in greater New Jersey and beyond.

With a wide range of academic programs and two main campuses in New Jersey, each with its own identity and separate character, the University offers the intimacy of a small college within a large suburban institution. The Florham-Madison Campus in Morris County has evolved into a traditional liberal arts environment, with a largely full-time residential student population. It also provides specialized graduate programs. Offering a full complement of undergraduate and graduate programs, the Teaneck-Hackensack Campus features genuine diversity in student ethnicity, age range, and skill level. There is a strong career focus with numerous professionally accredited graduate and certificate programs.

FDU was founded in 1942 as a two-year institution in Rutherford, when the available choices for acquiring higher education in New Jersey were few. FDU made higher education possible for thousands of the state's residents, and the school grew rapidly, becoming a four-year institution and a major multicampus university. The University today offers approximately 100 undergraduate and graduate degree programs leading to associate's, baccalaureate, master's, and doctoral degrees in the arts and sciences, as well as degrees and certificates in professional fields. The University is distinguished by many programs. For example, FDU is a well-known center for advanced business education, having one of the largest MBA programs in the country and earning national recognition for its programs in accounting and entrepreneurial studies.

The Teaneck-Hackensack Campus.

Opened in 1958, the Florham-Madison Campus is a beautifully landscaped park of approximately 164 acres and was known as "Florham" when it was created as an estate for Florence Vanderbilt Twombly and Hamilton Twombly. The landscape was planned by Frederick Law Olmsted, who is renowned as the designer of New York City's Central Park. The estate's principal buildings, designed in Georgian style in the 1890s, have been adapted for educational use. The 100-room Mansion, centerpiece of the campus, is a replica of a wing in King Henry VIII's Hampton Court. FDU recently constructed a recreation center, academic building, and residence hall, all designed in conformity with the campus's architectural heritage.

FDU has long made global education a cornerstone of its mission. In England, the University owns and operates Wroxton College, near Oxford, while in Israel FDU operates a branch campus in Tel Aviv. Also, the University has developed programs and cooperative agreements with institutions in Spain, Russia, Korea, and Thailand, among others. Approximately 800 students from more than 60 countries study at FDU.

The Mansion at the Florham-Madison Campus.

Especially significant is the impact the University has had and continues to have on the New Jersey economy. FDU has enjoyed a rich history of providing the state with knowledgeable, creative business leadership. More than 1,000 FDU graduates hold the titles chief executive officer, chief financial officer, chief operating officer, president, or vice president or are the proprietors of their own New Jersey businesses.

Under the leadership of its new president, J. Michael Adams, FDU is poised to build on its history, accomplishments, and advantages. It has recently declared a new mission "dedicated to the preparation of world citizens through global education" and designed to "provide students with the multidisciplinary, intercultural, and ethical understandings necessary to participate, lead, and prosper in the global marketplace of ideas, commerce, and culture." ☐

Anthony's PIZZA & PASTA
WE DELIVER
PIZZA PASTA BURGERS
HOPSTICK HOUSE CHINESE RESTAURANT
STUDIO

10

Health Care and Quality of Life

Photo by L. A. Popp.

Morristown Memorial Hospital— Atlantic Health System

From conception to the prime years of life, Atlantic Health System's Morristown Memorial Hospital has been meeting the health care needs of the people in Morris County and surrounding communities for more than 100 years.

According to historical records, "The pluck and determination of scores of people, clergy, doctors, business owners, even young children" helped build Morristown Memorial.

A bird's-eye view of Morristown Memorial Hospital, the second largest employer in Morris County with more than 4,000 full- and part-time employees.

That same spirit of determination remains steadfast today, resulting in a vibrant environment where world-class health-care professionals merge technology and medicine with the human touch to heal, offer hope, and enhance human life.

Currently, Morristown Memorial is the largest employer in Morristown and the second largest employer in Morris County. About 4,000 full- and part-time employees staff the nonprofit community hospital, including some of the region's finest physicians with expertise in dozens of medical and surgical specialties and subspecialties.

Morristown Memorial is one of four hospitals that are part of Atlantic Health System, one of the largest health-care systems in the state, providing health-care services for people in 11 counties in northern and central New Jersey. The other hospitals within the system include Overlook Hospital in Summit, Mountainside Hospital in Montclair/Glen Ridge, and The General Hospital Center at Passaic.

Each year, close to 25,000 people are admitted to Morristown Memorial, and nearly 4,000 babies are born at the hospital every year.

Whether patients' needs are cautionary, chronic, or critical, chances are they will find the care they require at Morristown Memorial. The hospital offers specialized services in cardiology and cardiac surgery, adult and pediatric oncology, critical and emergency care, inpatient rehabilitation services, obstetrics, and neonatal intensive care services. Morristown Memorial is a Level II trauma center, regional perinatal center, and a regional pediatric center. It operates the largest photopheresis (a treatment for lymphoma approved by the U.S. Food and Drug Administration) center in the United States and the only one in New Jersey.

"Morristown Memorial is also a major teaching hospital affiliated with the University of Medicine and Dentistry of New Jersey," said Marvin O'Quinn, executive vice president, Morristown Memorial Hospital and Overlook Hospital. "We have more than 100 resident physicians in training."

Targeting Disease through Specialty Centers

Morristown Memorial provides numerous specialty centers that enable residents to receive high-quality care close to home.

The Carol G. Simon Cancer Center offers advanced methods to diagnose, treat, and manage all types of cancer. The center's mission emphasizes "comprehensive and compassionate individualized treatment to our patients." Upon entering the center, the edict is reflected in both the cool, clean, high-tech equipment and the warm, soothing environment that embraces each individual who utilizes the center.

Patients have access to world-class oncology specialists and the latest technological innovations in diagnostic and treatment options. For example, Morristown Memorial physicians were among the first in the country to unveil the nation's first Siemens CT-on-Rails/Linear Accelerator, which provides oncologists with accurate, virtual real-time diagnostic-quality images of tumors within the treatment room.

"The CT-on-Rails/Linac System represents an extraordinary breakthrough in the field of radiation therapy," said James R. Wong, M.D., chairman of Radiation Oncology at Morristown Memorial Hospital. "The system allows the patient to remain on one table while his/her tumor is pinpointed and treatment is more accurately delivered. Current procedures require the patient to be relocated from a diagnosis area to the treatment table, increasing the potential for the tumor and/or internal organs to move.

More than 25,000 people a year are admitted to Morristown Memorial. Photo by Rene Perez.

The Carol G. Simon Cancer Center is also home to a number of specialty cancer programs. The Women's Cancer Center is designed for women who are being treated for uterine, ovarian, cervical, and other gynecologic cancers. The Peter B. Doherty Men's Cancer Program provides care for bladder, kidney, prostate, and testicular cancers. The hospital's children's cancer program was recently named a Valerie Fund Center—one of six in New Jersey. The Valerie Fund supports treatment for children with cancer and blood disorders, such as leukemia, lymphoma, brain, and other tumors.

Cancer care is further enhanced at Morristown Memorial by Atlantic Health System's partnership with The Cancer Institute of New Jersey (CINJ)—a university-based cancer research and patient-care network. At any one time, physicians at Morristown Memorial are involved in more than 70 regional and national research protocols for new cancer treatments offered through CINJ, as well as numerous other cancer-related groups.

The Center for Cardiovascular Disease is another premier service at Morristown Memorial, providing extensive cardiac surgical procedures, such as coronary bypass surgery, minimally invasive coronary surgery, valve replacement, and repairs and major aortic surgery, plus comprehensive cardiac diagnostic services.

"The New Jersey Department of Health has repeatedly ranked the hospital a leader in both the number of cardiac surgeries and best in observed survival rates," according to O'Quinn. At Morristown Memorial, cardiac surgeons perform more than 1,600 open-heart procedures a year. "In cardiac surgery, experience equals success," said Grant V. S. Parr, M.D., chief of cardiovascular surgery, Atlantic Health System. "Since our program was established, we have made a real commitment to quality." So much so that the hospital was ranked among the Top 100 Cardiovascular Hospitals in the country and the only one in New Jersey by the HCIA-Sachs Institute.

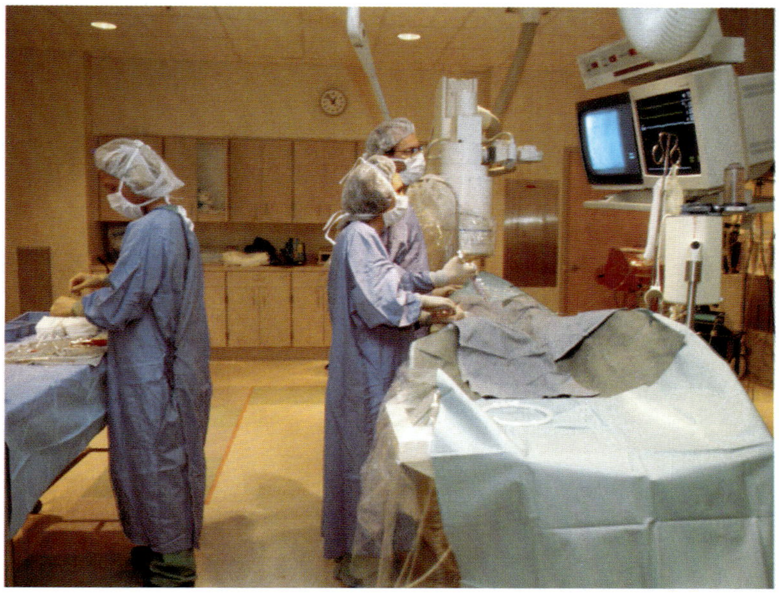

In the Cardiac Cath Lab, a team prepares for cardiac catheterization.

Services at the Center for Cardiovascular Disease include invasive cardiology and noninvasive cardiology. Some examples of invasive cardiology include cardiac catheterization (allows the physician to see blockages in arteries and other abnormalities), angioplasty (expands the clogged artery to increase blood flow), coronary stenting (holds the coronary artery open during angioplasty), and electrophysiology (finds abnormalities responsible for arrhythmias). Noninvasive cardiology includes adult echocardiography (takes pictures of the heart using sound waves), Holter monitoring (monitors heart rhythms), stress tests (records the heart's response during exercise), and electrocardiography (records electrical activity of the heart), to name a few. The hospital also includes a Pacemaker Evaluation Center and a Cardiac Health Center to promote prevention and wellness.

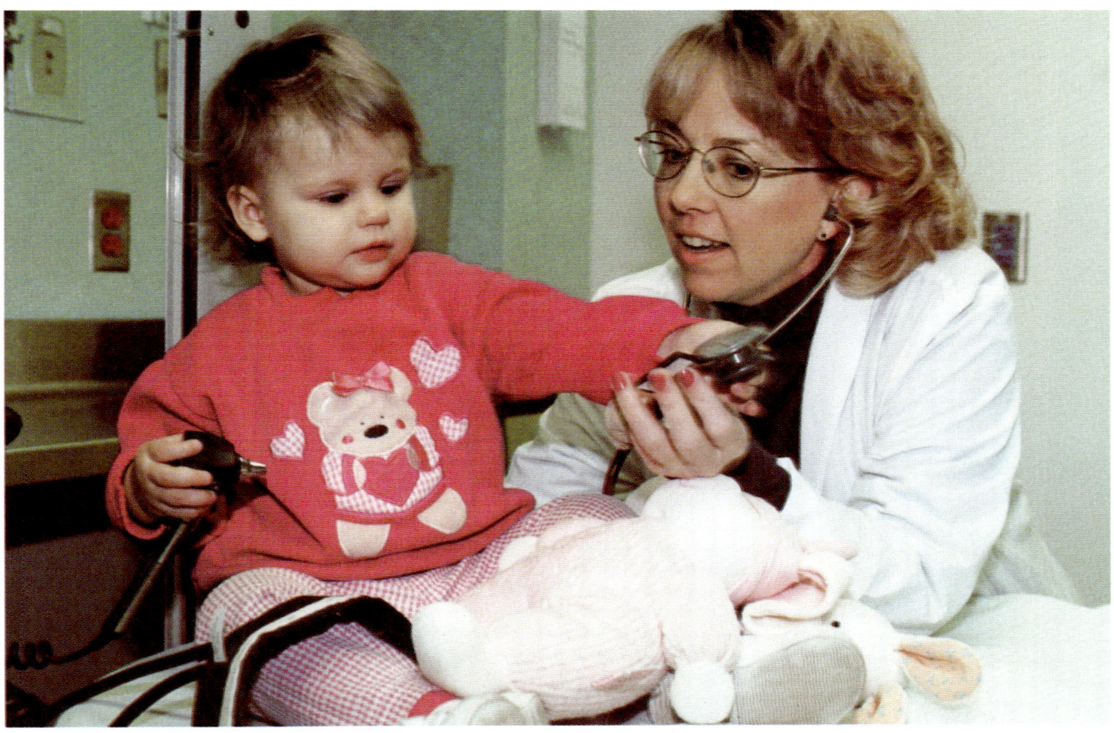

A pediatric nurse cares for a child in the hospital's Pediatric Emergency Department.

For about 20 years, the School of Cardiovascular Technology has thrived at Morristown Memorial. The two-year program prepares students to become registered cardiovascular technologists in one of three specialties: invasive cardiology, noninvasive cardiology, and peripheral vascular diagnostics.

Through its membership in Atlantic Health System, Morristown Memorial also participates in national and international research studies that contribute to advancements in the prevention, early detection, and treatment of cardiovascular disease.

Pediatric care is another growing service at Morristown Memorial. In 1999, the hospital unveiled plans to build a new Children's Medical Center to "bring all pediatric services into one convenient, child-friendly location," said Leonard Feld, M.D., chairman of the department of pediatrics, Atlantic Health System. The $31-million project will feature the Goryeb Children's Center, which will include a Day Hospital for same-day procedures and clinical research, the Valerie Fund Center for children with cancer and blood disorders, a diabetes center, diagnostic center, and special care unit for critically ill or injured young people. A children's inpatient unit will also be part of the new Children's Medical Center. This unit will include private rooms designed to accommodate parents' overnight stays.

In addition, the new Children's Medical Center Project also includes the construction of the Gagnon Children's Emergency Center adjacent to the adult emergency department, which will include eight treatment rooms and a separate waiting area.

One of the hospital's newest endeavors is the Ambulatory Surgery Center. Located across the street from the main hospital building, the Ambulatory Surgery Center provides same-day surgery patients of all ages with quality surgical care. The facility is equipped with six operating rooms with ceiling mounted video systems and the latest technology and computerized equipment. About 10,000 surgeries a year will be performed in the Ambulatory Surgery Center.

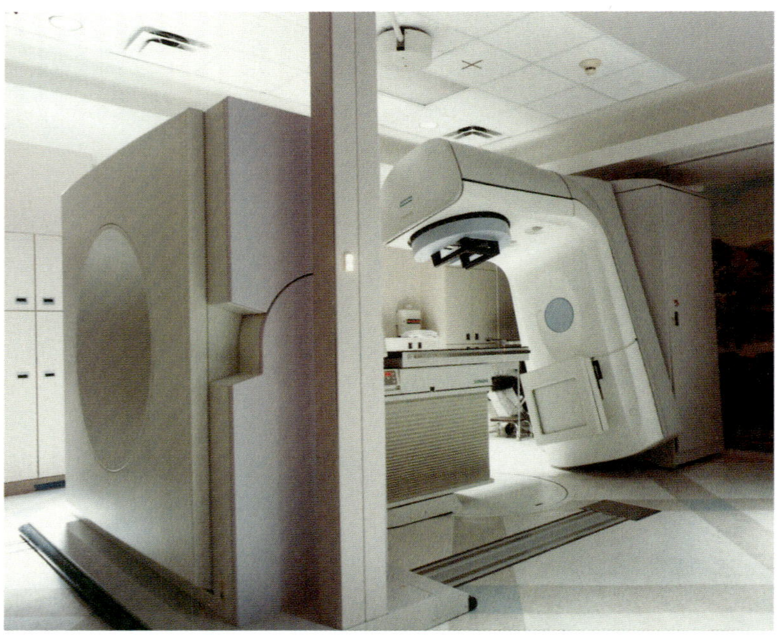

At the Carol G. Simon Cancer Center, radiation specialists utilize the country's first Siemens CT-on-Rails/ Linear Accelerator, which provides oncologists with accurate, virtual real-time diagnostic-quality images of tumors within the treatment room.

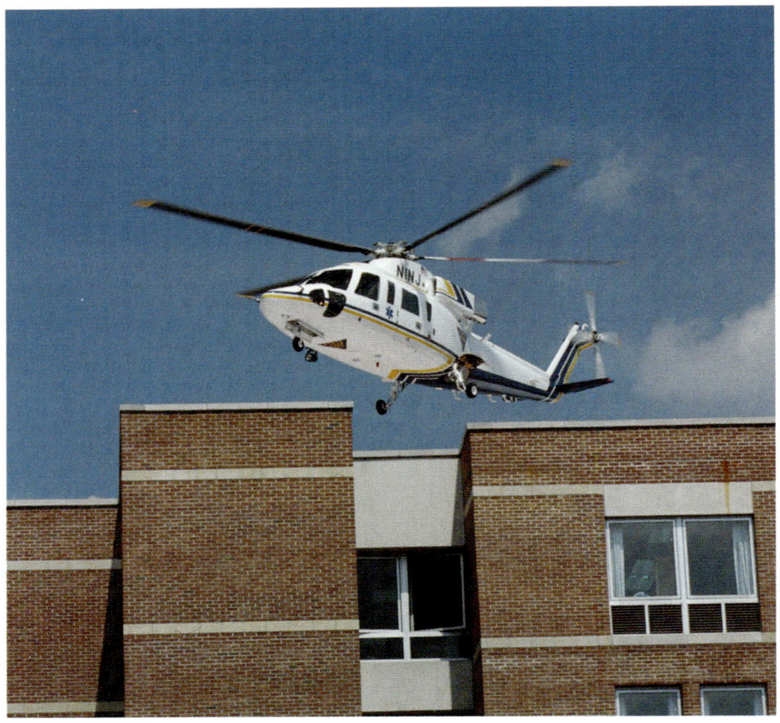

A helicopter prepares for landing at the rooftop heliport, which provides easy access to the hospital's Trauma Center. Photo by Rene Perez.

"New advances in technology and equipment, and the continued growth in the number of same-day surgical procedures performed at Morristown Memorial each year, made it necessary for the hospital to expand its ambulatory surgical services," said Gerald Lefever, M.D., medical director, Ambulatory Surgery Center. "This newly refurbished facility offers patients the comfort and privacy of a same-day setting coupled with Morristown Memorial's renowned surgical expertise."

Located within the Ambulatory Surgery Center is the Pain Management Center, where physicians treat acute post-operative pain, chronic neck and back pain, peripheral nerve pain, and cancer pain. Special programs for headache and fibromyalgia are also in development.

The hospital also provides a number of emergency services. Morristown Memorial is a regional trauma center with a multidisciplinary trauma team, a 43-bed orthopedic surgical trauma unit, a 25-bed emergency department, an injury prevention program to provide education to children and adults, an 18-bed intensive care unit, a mobile intensive care unit, a surgical step-down unit, a respiratory spinal care unit, and a rooftop heliport that enables quick delivery and transfer of patients.

Atlantic's Rehabilitation Institute offers comprehensive inpatient and outpatient services, such as an audiology and hearing aid center, handicapped driver evaluation and training, a mild brain injury program, and therapeutic pool/aquatic rehabilitation programs.

The hospital offers niche services, too, such as the Sleep Disorder Center, the Wound Care Center, Obesity Center, Hyperbaric Medicine Program, the Arthritis Center, and the Diabetes Center. Atlantic's Mind Body Center gives patients access to therapies like acupuncture, massage and reflexology, yoga, hypnosis, meditation, homeopathy, and spiritual interventions such as prayer and healing.

An artist's rendering of the proposed Goryeb Children's Center, which will include: a Day Hospital for same-day procedures and clinical research, the Valerie Fund Center for children with cancer and blood disorders, a diabetes center, diagnostic center, and special care unit for critically ill or injured young people.

Promoting a Healthier Community

Morristown Memorial reaches deep into the community with free programs and services designed to help residents take charge of and improve their health.

"Improving community health is at the core of all Morristown Memorial Hospital's services; it guides our mission and vision," said O'Quinn. "Throughout the year, we sponsor or take part in many community health activities."

For example, Community Health Day: A Family Day of Wellness is a free event sponsored by the hospital in cooperation with local churches and other organizations. The day includes asthma, blood pressure, cholesterol and cancer screenings, health exhibits, and a mobile dental van.

The Teen Health Web site, TeenHealthFX is funded by the hospital as part of a joint initiative with community leaders. The web site is a place where young people can find answers to their health-related questions and talk openly about mental and physical well-being.

Pro-Kids is a program initiated by the hospital's Volunteer Department in conjunction with the Children's Medical Center. Pro-Kids offers a variety of programs from nutritional information to educating kids about the dangers of alcohol and drugs.

For senior citizens, the hospital boasts one of the largest Senior Contact programs, providing health screenings and lectures for people who are 60 years of age and older.

Building for the Future

To stay on top of patients' health-care needs, Morristown Memorial continuously upgrades and expands its services and facilities. Currently, several expansion programs have been initiated.

The hospital's Intensive Care Unit, which treats more than 1,300 patients a year, recently expanded and renovated to include a more modern, comfortable environment for patients and their families, as well as added privacy," said O'Quinn. It houses 22 private patient rooms and a family waiting area and overnight accommodations for the patients' visitors.

And, once constructed, the new Children's Medical Center will bring all pediatric services into one child-friendly location within an 88,000-square-foot facility expected to open in early 2002.

"The physicians and staff of Morristown Memorial Hospital are committed to meeting the health-care needs of the people in the communities around us," said O'Quinn. "We provide the most advanced technology and services, and our physicians are trained and educated at the finest institutions. Our patients can find it all right here." □

Local teens try out the new Teen Health Web site funded by Morristown Memorial Hospital in a joint initiative with community leaders. The Web site gives young adults a place to go to find answers to their difficult-to-ask health questions.

American Home Products Corporation

American Home Products' portfolio of human and animal health care products contains some of the most recognized brands in the world, such as Premarin®, Advil® and Centrum®. In addition to this exciting lineup of products, American Home Products (AHP) continues to search for new medicines that treat some of the most debilitating and serious health conditions in the world.

"We're investing about $2 billion in research and development of new products," says John Stafford, chairman and chief executive officer. "That investment is double the amount we spent five years ago, which clearly demonstrates our long-term commitment to research and development."

The American Home Products facility within the 310-acre Giralda Farms corporate park.

Founded in 1926, AHP is one of the largest research-based pharmaceutical and health care products companies in the world. It is a leader in the discovery, development, manufacturing, and marketing of prescription drugs and over-the-counter medications. It is also a leader in vaccines, biotechnology, and animal health care.

Previously based in New York City, in 1993, AHP moved its corporate headquarters into a 450,000-square-foot facility within the scenic Giralda Farms corporate park in Madison, New Jersey which houses about 1,000 employees. Overall, about 3,000 employees are based in New Jersey and worldwide, AHP has approximately 47,000 employees with companies operating in more than 100 countries.

Recently, AHP was listed in *Industry Week* as among the top 100 best-managed companies in the world. The AHP family structure includes three core, operating units: Wyeth-Ayerst Pharmaceuticals, Whitehall-Robins Healthcare, and Fort Dodge Animal Health. Each operating unit has specialty areas of focus, giving AHP far-reaching expertise in a variety of health care areas.

In prescription products, Wyeth-Ayerst has leading products in the areas of women's health care, cardiovascular therapies, central-nervous-system drugs, musculoskeletal therapies, infectious disease, hemophilia, oncology, vaccines, and generic pharmaceuticals. Cornerstone products include Premarin®, Effexor® XR, and Enbrel®.

Special units within Wyeth-Ayerst include Wyeth Lederle Vaccines, a supplier of adults' and childrens' vaccines that prevent diseases such as diphtheria, influenza, meningitis, pneumonia, and whooping cough; and Genetics Institute, which is engaged in the discovery, development, and commercialization of human pharmaceuticals through recombinant DNA, genomics, and other technologies. AHP's pharmaceutical research and development combines the research efforts of Wyeth-Ayerst Research and Genetics Institute.

"Because of our intensive research efforts and strategic alliances, we've recently launched a number of new and exciting products including Enbrel for moderate to severe rheumatoid arthritis, Sonata for the short-term treatment of insomnia in adults, including elderly patients, and Rapamune for the prevention of organ rejection following renal transplantation," says Stafford. "Our pipeline is full of many additional break-through pharmaceutical products, which positions us for even stronger growth in the future."

In the area of over-the-counter consumer products, Whitehall-Robins Healthcare researches, develops, manufactures, and markets consumer health care products. The company's products are focused on four therapeutic areas: analgesics, nutritionals, respiratory remedies, and gastrointestinal/topical products. Many of the company's products, such as Advil®, Chap Stick®, Centrum®, and Robitussin®, are leaders in their respective categories.

Within the Whitehall-Robins Healthcare Division is Solgar Vitamin and Herb, a leading authority in nutritional science, technology, and education. As one of the industry's oldest and most respected researchers and manufacturers of premium nutritional supplements, Solgar offers more than 400 nutritional supplements, distributing to health-food retailers in the U.S. and abroad.

Whitehall-Robins Healthcare offers some of the world's best-known and most-trusted over-the-counter (OTC) medications. The company's status in the OTC industry is impressive: it holds a leadership position worldwide in OTC sales and has three of the top 10 OTC brands in the United States. An aggressive new product effort, coupled with sales of *Solgar* products, propelled Whitehall-Robins to a record performance in 1999.

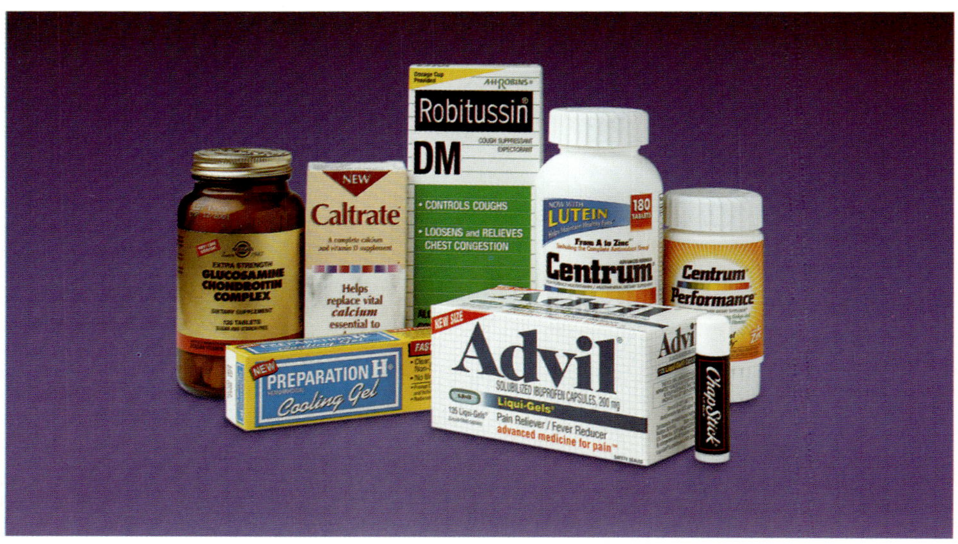

In the area of animal health care, Fort Dodge Animal Health manufactures and distributes prescription and over-the-counter animal health-care products for the livestock, companion animal, swine, and poultry industries in North America and international markets. Key products include CYDECTIN® Pour-On for parasite control in cattle, QUEST® Gel dewormer and boticide for horses, and EtoGesic® Tablets for osteoarthritis pain relief in dogs.

AHP's impact on human and animal health is visible around the world. It is also evident close to home, in Morris County, where employees contribute their time and talents to improve life within the local community. Throughout the year, AHP employees provide hands-on volunteer support for United Way agencies like the Morris Shelter, Morris County Head Start, and the Madison Community House. For years, the company has sponsored the AHP 5K Run with Pride at Giralda Farms to benefit Project Community Pride, a program of volunteer community service for juvenile offenders.

The Company provides support for programs and projects related to health care, education, the arts, business and civic activities, and social services. Numerous agencies benefit from AHP funding, including the American Red Cross, Arthritis Foundation, Boys & Girls Clubs of America, The Children's Health Fund, UNCF/The College Fund, The Colonial Symphony, Inroads, Lincoln Center, Morristown Memorial Hospital, National Osteoporosis Foundation, National Center on Addiction and Substance Abuse, United Cerebral Palsy, and United Way. For its outstanding community support, AHP has been awarded the Kellogg Award from the United Way of Morris County.

In addition to providing support to the community, AHP believes it is important to give employees the support they need. The Madison site contains numerous convenient services and facilities, such as a company store, dry cleaning services, a health and fitness center, extracurricular sporting activities, and peaceful jogging, biking, and walking trails threaded throughout Giralda Farms.

To show its support for families, AHP offers employees dependent care financial assistance and adoption assistance benefits. Many employees have an annual opportunity to choose their daily work schedules for greater flexibility. A state-of-the-art onsite Child Development Center helps employees fulfill their childcare needs. Multiple times, AHP has been named one of the best companies for working mothers by *Working Mother* magazine.

"AHP is committed to its employees, providing work/life programs and policies that assist them in balancing work and family responsibilities," says Stafford. "We are also committed to our responsibility of providing innovative products that continue to improve life and health for communities around the world." □

A Wyeth-Ayerst scientist in the lab.

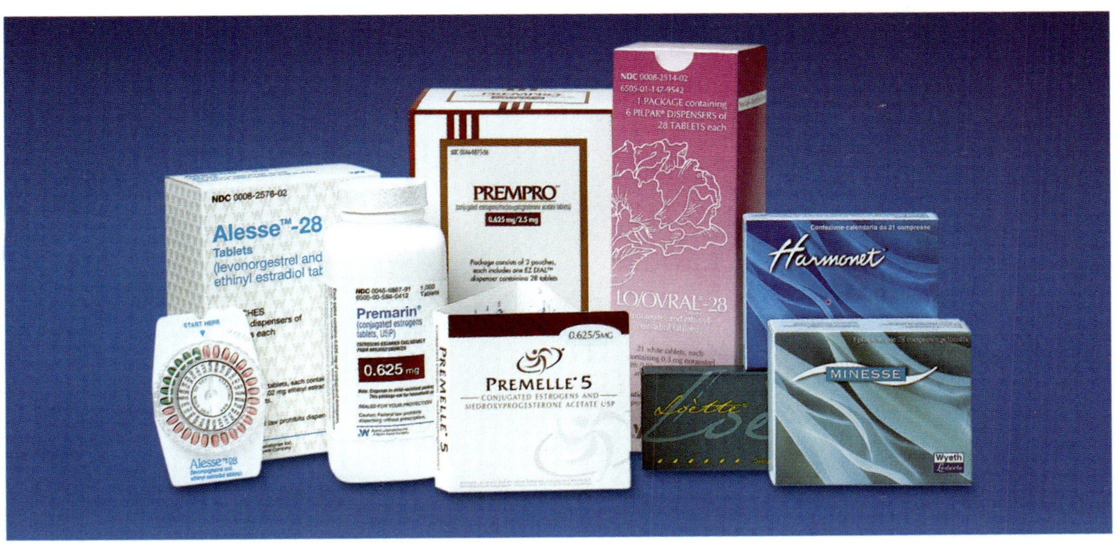

Wyeth-Ayerst is the worldwide leader in women's health care. Its Women's Health Research Institute remains at the forefront of new discoveries on the role of estrogen in a woman's body throughout her life. The benefits of this experience and leadership are clearly demonstrated in the growth of the *Premarin* family of products, the most prescribed hormone replacement therapies in the world, and *Alesse*, the top selling 20 microgram birth control pill in the United States.

National Prescription Administrators, Inc.

National Prescription Administrators, Inc. (NPA), the nation's largest truly independent prescription benefit management company, sets industry standards with superior customer service and utilization management serving 7-million lives with flexible benefit design and plan management, integrated mail order pharmacy, leading-edge eligibility and information technology, as well as clinical, and utilization management programs.

From its founding as a pharmacist-owned, independent prescription benefit manager (PBM) in 1978, NPA has grown from three employees to be the number-one PBM in the nation through an operating philosophy of outstanding customer service.

The 22-year-old privately held company moved 400 employees to a new landmark site in East Hanover, New Jersey in 1994. NPA's 253,000 square feet of offices stand as a statement of its commitment to growth and to a new level of service for its sponsoring organizations. The award-winning structure of steel and glass, with its 77,000-square-foot warehouse and 24 departments, rises three floors overlooking 20 acres of property. An open tree-lined courtyard graces the view from the light-filled cafeteria.

In serving its sponsors, NPA is really serving patients and their many needs. NPA's provider of vision benefit services, National Vision Administrators (NVA), which is also located in East Hanover, shares space at NPA's headquarters. In addition, the spacious East Hanover facilities house Central Fill, Inc. (CFI), NPA's preferred Mail Pharmacy provider. CFI's cutting-edge Rx mail service operation is fully automated and boasts of a mirror facility in Harrisburg, Pennsylvania.

Within five years of the move to East Hanover, NPA rose from number one in the nation in Customer Service to become the number one PBM for Overall Service and Performance in 17 categories in an independent survey of employers by the Pharmacy Benefit Management Institute. These employers are the sponsors of prescription benefit plans throughout the nation.

With over 950 employees, NPA's Morris County culture has become as diverse as its clients which include the United Federation of Teachers Welfare Fund, Hershey Foods, and the State of Illinois Bureau of Benefits. In the most recent independent survey of employers in 2000, NPA was again voted the number one PBM in the nation for the fourth year straight. And, NPA has consistently held the lead in Customer Service for six years in a row—since the survey began.

In any industry, the most successful companies everywhere hold an underlying key belief about keeping customers happy. NPA has served its sponsors over the years with one driving value: prescription care that keeps plan members healthy and productive.

"NPA's success thrives upon sensitive collaboration with our sponsors in designing and creating flexible prescription plans that offer them the very best quality and value," says pharmacist Richard O. Ullman, R.Ph., NPA's President and founder. The partnership NPA has with each client is truly an ongoing survey because we continuously ask them what they want and need. We devote ourselves to exceeding their expectations."

If NPA's unbiased judgment regarding client care sounds like a love story, that's because it is. Integrity is the motivating

National Prescription Administrators has consistently been number one in the nation for customer service in the independent survey of employers by the Pharmacy Benefit Management Institute.

concern across NPA's broad array of programs. NPA's customer-acclaimed prescription benefit customer services are enjoyed by more than 600 major corporations, union groups, insurance companies, government organizations, and HMOs.

Benefits such as 24-hour turnaround on its customers' prescription cards, seamless up-to-the-minute electronic eligibility, and custom plan designs are clear examples of NPA's customer-driven focus. NPA also helps pharmacists to help the patient by providing real-time eligibility information as well as on-line clinical utilization management information. This increases pharmacy efficiency, and enhances patient satisfaction.

NPA offers comprehensive clinical and utilization management. In addition to drug utilization on-line edits, NPA's clinical pharmacists personally review and intervene upon thousands of situations in the areas of fraud, drug abuse, inappropriate therapy, and inefficient prescribing habits. This is a time-intensive, resource-consuming process which again and again demonstrates NPA's commitment to the extras that bear proof to their credo, "prescription care with your benefit in mind."

But NPA's concern for the patient and the control of health care expenses doesn't stop with the care of the client and the plan member. Every Wednesday, NPA employees assist the local East Hanover First Aid Squad in providing auxiliary Emergency Response for neighboring towns, which saves New Jersey taxpayers thousands of dollars each year. In fact, NPA was the first employer within the community to take an active role in East Hanover's Adopt-a-Day Emergency Response Program.

First also to recognize the key role of the pharmacist in the health care delivery system, NPA fully understands the need to preserve the future of pharmacy in today's buyer-driven health care revolution. "The pharmacist is the most trusted professional in our nation," Ullman notes. "They are always there for the patient. Pharmacists are the trained experts who provide the right combination of availability, skills, and knowledge. NPA's focus is on Quality, the best and the most economical use of pharmaceuticals through pharmacists."

NPA continues to earn its position as an industry leader fostering thoughtful cooperation between pharmacist, physician, and patient. Ullman adds, "NPA wants pharmacists to remain in the business of taking care of patients and we want them to thrive at this. With the skyrocketing costs of new lifesaving and life-enhancing drugs, the future of patient care for all of us is linked to the integrity of prescription care. This can only be possible through the preservation of the pivotal role of the community pharmacist. People have to take care of people." □

In 1994, NPA moved to a new landmark site in East Hanover, New Jersey, featuring 253,000 square feet of office space. The award-winning structure of steel and glass stands as a statement of NPA's commitment to growth and to a new level of service for its sponsoring organizations.

The Seeing Eye

With head held high, harness in hand, and a gentle Labrador retriever as her guide, a blind woman maneuvers the streets of New York City, undaunted by the noise, the traffic, and bustling crowds around her.

She is one of thousands of graduates of The Seeing Eye, a school in Morris County that has been enhancing the independence, dignity, and self-confidence of people who are blind and visually impaired for more than 70 years.

The Seeing Eye is the first and oldest dog guide school in America, founded in 1929 in Nashville. In 1931, The Seeing Eye moved to Whippany in Morris County, and it has been located on 70 acres near downtown Morristown since 1965.

"The Seeing Eye is not just about dogs," says Kenneth Rosenthal, president of The Seeing Eye. "It's about people and dogs and the many things they can do together."

The Seeing Eye is the first and oldest dog guide school in America. It was founded in 1929 in Nashville by Dorothy Harrison Eustis, who was fascinated with the intelligence of German shepherds, and Morris Frank, who became the first blind person in America to use a dog guide. In 1931, The Seeing Eye moved to Whippany in Morris County and has been located on 70 acres near downtown Morristown since 1965.

Over the past 70 years, more than 12,000 specially bred and trained dog guides have been matched with blind people throughout the United States and Canada. Today, nearly 1,700 graduates lead productive, independent lives with Seeing Eye® dogs. Their success stories are the result of careful canine breeding, time-tested training, and unlimited love from the volunteers and instructors dedicated to helping blind people achieve more mobile lives.

Annually, hundreds of German shepherds, Labrador retrievers, and Golden retrievers are born at The Seeing Eye Scientific Breeding Station in Mendham a few miles from the main campus. Careful genetic monitoring and tracking ensure that the puppies are healthy and have the right temperament, intelligence, and trainability to become a dog guide. In 2000, The Seeing Eye broke ground in Chester Township for a 61,000-square-foot breeding facility to house up to 90 dogs and produce up to 108 litters per year.

Once the puppies reach eight weeks old, they are placed with volunteer families through the Seeing Eye Puppy Raising/4-H Program. Each year, more than 600 families from New Jersey, Pennsylvania, and Delaware participate in the program. The puppies live with the families for about 18 months and learn basic obedience and socialization.

"Our puppy-raisers provide an invaluable service," says Mr. Rosenthal. "A dog raised in a kennel doesn't have the firm foundation of love and trust, or the wide exposure to different daily stimuli like traffic, pavement, and people, that a dog raised by a nurturing family in a home has."

After spending more than a year with a volunteer family, the puppies return to The Seeing Eye for four months of training with sighted instructors, each training about 10 dogs or a "string" at a time. They use a system of affectionate rewards and gentle corrections to teach each dog obedience and "intelligent disobedience," the ability to disregard a command if it would lead to danger.

"Strict obedience isn't what we're looking for," says Doug Roberts, director of programs. "A Seeing Eye dog must have a certain amount of freedom from heavy discipline, because he must be able to use reasoning power. He might have to figure out a way around a barricaded sidewalk in a big city or decide if it's safe to cross a street."

Under the Americans With Disabilities Act, dog guides are guaranteed access to enter all public places and accommodations, but dogs in training are not afforded the same rights. However, in downtown Morristown, where the community has embraced the mission of The Seeing Eye, it's not unusual to see a platoon of shepherds and retrievers in training, stopping at busy intersections, climbing escalators and moving through revolving doors. The dogs also go through training at places like Newark Airport, and bus and train stations.

At the end of the formal training program, the dogs are matched with blind people, and this new team trains together for 20 to 27 days. Once students receive their dogs, they live with them 24 hours a day while at The Seeing Eye. "This hastens the bonding between dog and master and helps solidify their working partnership," says Roberts.

Students spend between 20 and 27 days at The Seeing Eye learning how to use and care for their dogs. Currently, close to 1,700 graduates of The Seeing Eye live and work in the United States and Canada.

Seeing Eye Puppies are raised by volunteer families for about 18 months. At this time the dogs learn basic obedience and socialization in a nurturing environment that builds a foundation of love and trust not typically found in a kennel.

Students and their dogs first learn to work as teams in downtown Morristown. They master daily activities, such as going in and out of stores, using public transportation, and eating in restaurants. Later, trips are tailored to each student's specific needs. A city-dweller will learn to ride the subway with her dog. A country-dweller will learn to walk along streets without curbs.

A Seeing Eye instructor works with a string of ten dogs for a period of four months. In the fifth month the instructor becomes teacher to a blind student, offering instruction in the proper use and care of their new Seeing Eye® dog.

During it all, about 150 staff members and 100 volunteers spend countless hours providing health care for the dogs, managing the administrative functions of a philanthropic business, answering telephones, giving instructional tours for the public, and providing grooming, walking, and socialization activities for the dogs.

Throughout their stay at The Seeing Eye, students and their dogs are treated with the utmost care and respect. The same care is reflected in the buildings and grounds at The Seeing Eye. The facility includes the "House," which provides the residential wing for students, a dining room, lounge, and administrative offices; the Vincent A. Stabile Canine Health Center, which includes a veterinary clinic, kennel runs, office space, and library; the Walker Dillard Kirby Canine Center, which houses 120 dogs in training; and the Jenks House, which is home to various departments within The Seeing Eye.

Top-notch facilities and the highly motivated staff, volunteers, and students lead to successful results. But the public's cooperation is needed, too, explains Peter Lang, training manager. "When you see a dog guide working, there's a natural desire to talk to or pet these loyal, beautiful dogs. But petting or talking to a dog guide distracts it and its blind handler. This can create a dangerous situation for both."

"With the public's cooperation and support, we gain momentum for our mission of helping people who are blind," says Mr. Rosenthal.

Meanwhile, another litter is born—eight puppies this time. A van filled with new students arrives at the front door. And a graduate takes a final walk with her Seeing Eye dog along the quiet path that threads through the campus. It's the path to independence. □

Saint Clare's Health Services

From its beginnings in 1895, Saint Clare's Health Services has combined an enduring faith with the finest medical care to help create healthier communities.

Saint Clare's is a non-profit, Catholic health-care system that operates hospitals in Boonton Township, Denville, Dover, and Sussex Borough and community health centers at numerous satellite locations throughout the region. The system employs some 3,500 people, making it the fifth largest employer in Morris County and the seventh largest health-care provider in New Jersey. It has a medical staff of more than 700 physicians whose specialties range from pediatrics to neurosurgery. Throughout its various services and sites, an underlying mission unites all of Saint Clare's—a mission established by the Sisters of the Sorrowful Mother, who founded the system more than a century ago. That mission is to provide faith-based, quality health care for all people, regardless of financial status.

Saint Clare's is the New Jersey affiliate of the world-renowned Memorial Sloan-Kettering Cancer Center, named for six consecutive years by *U.S. News & World Report* as the nation's finest cancer center.

Each year, Saint Clare's admits 26,000 patients to its hospitals. Another 115,000 utilize outpatient services, such as same-day surgery, diagnostic testing, dialysis, diabetes treatment, and cardiac catheterization.

Because it is a true regional health-care system, Saint Clare's provides a range of services from neonatal care to senior care, from same-day surgery to long-term care, from emergency care to world-class cancer care.

"Being a regional health-care system allows us to meet the needs of both a growing and an aging community," said Kathryn J. McDonagh, president/chief executive officer. "In addition, our extensive community and corporate health programs allow us to partner with local businesses to provide education and health services to employees."

Saint Clare's is the New Jersey affiliate of the world-renowned Memorial Sloan-Kettering Cancer Center, named for six consecutive years by *U.S. News & World Report* as the nation's finest cancer center. "This affiliation allows us to provide world-class cancer care to our patients close to home," said McDonagh.

Other "centers of excellence" at Saint Clare's include five behavioral health centers throughout the region, a behavioral health hospital in Boonton Township, maternal- and child-health services that will include a newly renovated and expanded maternity center at Saint Clare's Hospital/Denville in 2001; specialized care for high-risk pregnancies and premature and sick newborns; cardiac diagnostics and treatment, and renal dialysis. Saint Clare's is the region's leading provider of cardiology testing services.

To respond to the needs of the aging population, in 1994, Saint Clare's opened Franciscan Oaks, a continuing-care retirement community on the Denville campus with 285 units for independent living, 33 assisted-living units, and 79 skilled-nursing beds. Also in Denville, Saint Clare's operates the St. Francis Residential Community for independent adults aged 65 and older.

In keeping with its mission to provide affordable, high-quality health care, Saint Clare's operates health centers in Morris and Sussex counties for Medicaid, charity-care, and low-income patients. For example, each year about 12,000 people visit the Community Health Center at Saint Clare's Hospital/Dover for pediatric, prenatal, and adult medical services.

To further demonstrate its commitment to the community, Saint Clare's provides ongoing educational programs, health screenings, and detection services. Each year, Saint Clare's health-care professionals teach CPR to an estimated 5,000 residents, host lecture series reaching some 2,500 people, sponsor health fairs for 1,200 children in local schools, screen about 5,500 older adults for hypertension, and conduct more than 100 cancer screenings across Morris County.

From world-class cancer care to specialized newborn care to devoted elder care, Saint Clare's remains committed to healing the body, mind, and spirit of the patients it serves. □

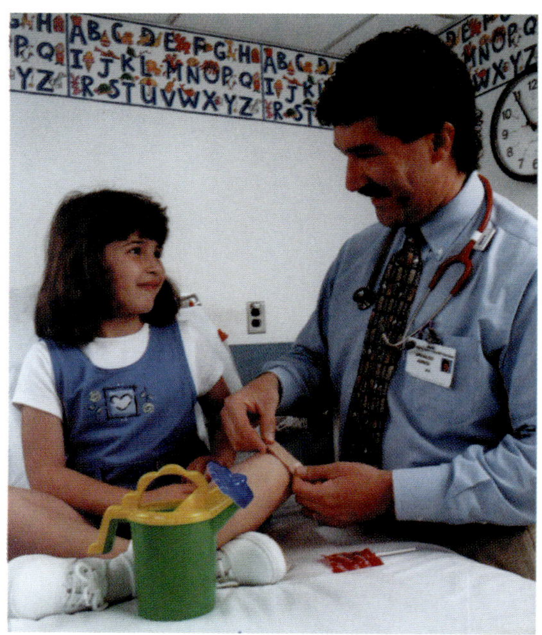

Saint Clare's has Morris County's only emergency service devoted exclusively to kids...the Evelyn M. Spiro Pediatric Emergency Care Center.

Heath Village

Tennis matches, poolside parties, computer clubs, and horse shows are all testament to the rhythm of life at Heath Village, one of New Jersey's finest retirement communities.

Heath Village is a non-profit, full-service retirement community located on the western slope of Schooley's Mountain in Washington Township. It is the second oldest retirement community in New Jersey and offers diverse care and activities for its 400 residents.

The Village's Porte Cochere offers an elegant and inviting welcome for residents and guests.

The community provides four levels of care, ranging from independent living to full-time nursing care. About 200 apartments and 10 cottages are available for independent living. Forty-eight hotel-style apartments offer supplementary services. A 40-bed residential health care facility provides 24-hour supervision. The 99-bed Clarence W. Sickles Health Care Center offers comprehensive nursing care. The Joint Commission on Accreditation of Healthcare Organizations (JCAHO) accredits the Clarence W. Sickles Health Care Center. This accreditation is considered the "Good Housekeeping" seal of approval for long-term-care facilities.

"Heath Village takes pride in its reputation for providing quality care, and we view accreditation as yet another step toward excellence," says Patrick Brady, executive director.

In addition to varying levels of care, Heath Village has more than 25 resident groups on campus. For example, a men's woodworking group has built a pirate ship for the Friendship Center, an intergenerational childcare facility located on the Heath Village grounds. At the Friendship Center, seniors interact with children in an array of activities, from nature walks to language class. There is also a computer club, which recently developed an Internet correspondence system for one of the residents, whose family was on a deep-sea expedition to New Zealand in search of giant squid.

A lighted tennis court provides plenty of opportunity for friendly competition.

From hiking and biking to golf and gardening, Heath Village is a "home for all seasons," says Betsi Olmstead, public relations/development coordinator. "It's a friendly, affordable place to live. We offer a unique financial agreement, a pay-as-you-go system, with affordable monthly rates and modest entrance fees."

About 250 part-time and full-time employees staff the retirement community. Many have worked at Heath Village for more than two decades. Along with housekeeping and maintenance staff, there are nurses, dieticians, and therapists in the physical therapy and rehabilitation department. Local doctors, such as podiatrists and ophthalmologists, offer onsite services. Residents also have access to an adult daycare facility located just across the street.

"Seniors today are more active than ever. They like variety. They like challenges" says Olmstead. "Heath Village provides an absolutely beautiful setting bursting with activities for our seniors."

The retirement village is also preparing for seniors in the future. Long-range expansion plans include the development of a new adult lifestyle community across the street. Heath Alliance for Care Inc., the parent company for Heath Village, is in the process of purchasing 113 acres for future construction of the River Valley Farms Adult Lifestyle Community.

When 2011 rolls around, so will the first wave of baby boomers turning 65. Many of them will be looking for a safe, affordable place to call home. Heath Village will be ready. ☐

11

Real Estate and Development

Photo by L. A. Popp.

Elite Corporate Housing

Morris County businesses represent almost every industry imaginable, from metal manufacturers to medicine makers. Despite their diversity, these growing businesses often face a similar task: They must find temporary, appropriate housing for their influx of workers.

One company, Elite Corporate Housing, has been helping Morris County businesses address their employees' temporary housing needs since 1997. Founded by Jay Favia, an entrepreneur and long-time participant in the housing industry, Elite Corporate Housing is a niche company that provides short-term furnished apartments for the increasing number of new employees and temporary contract workers entering Morris County industries.

Headquarters and major facilities for about 10 percent of the Fortune 500 are located within Morris County. Elite Corporate Housing partners with many of them, including pharmaceutical, telecommunications, and chemical companies. These thriving companies often recruit new employees, transfer existing employees to Morris County from other regions, or bring in employees on temporary assignments. In each scenario, companies often need to find their workers temporary places to live. Some companies choose to place a worker in a hotel for one to three months, but this can be expensive and inconvenient for a worker who stays months at a time. Others call on Elite Corporate Housing.

Elite Corporate Housing manages about 200 apartments, predominately in Morris County. Because of the proximity to New York, Elite Corporate Housing also finds apartments for employees who prefer to live in Manhattan and commute to Morris County. Apartments range from $1,750 a month to $4,000 a month, depending on the individual's requirements.

Companies rely on Elite Corporate Housing because the knowledgeable staff can provide apartments that are affordable and reflective of employees' lifestyles. It's not uncommon in Morris County for companies to hire college or summer interns for three to six months. These interns have highly specific needs, and Elite Corporate Housing helps match interns with apartments that meet those needs. For example, many interns need public transportation because they do not have a car. They also prefer to live in areas where there is access to lots of culture, nightlife, and young people in similar situations. Elite Corporate Housing caters to each of these requirements.

Under other circumstances, Elite Corporate Housing may need to provide an apartment for a senior manager who is having a house built. The senior manager may have

Photo by L. A. Popp.

Photo by L. A. Popp.

children who will require additional space, or the executive may desire a more high-end apartment where he or she can entertain clients and co-workers.

About 60 percent of Elite Corporate Housing's renters are on business from outside of the U.S. because many corporations within Morris County are involved in global business activities. There are also growing numbers of renters moving into the county from the computer industry. The introduction of new technology requires that more computer specialists move into the area, and many are on temporary assignments. They help Morris County businesses develop new systems, implement them, and train employees to use them. These temporary workers may be in the area for 30 days or up to 90 days. Because their assignments are deadline oriented, they often face high-pressure situations with tight deadlines. Again, Elite Corporate Housing provides them with a place that fits their specific needs—often, a quiet place where they can unwind at the end of the day.

Each of Elite Corporate Housing's apartments is in move-in condition, which means the cable and telephone are hooked up, and the apartment is clean and equipped with appliances and new or like-new furniture.

Elite Corporate Housing's staff members include maintenance and cleaning crews and bookkeeping staff. Overhead costs are kept to a minimum, which allows Elite Corporate Housing to pass on savings to its cost-conscientious clients.

Along with competitive pricing, Elite Corporate Housing offers its clients the highest level of customer service in the housing industry. Responsiveness and attentiveness are priorities at Elite Corporate Housing. When companies call Elite Corporate Housing, they know they will receive a response within 24 hours or less. They also know their employees will be treated with respect and courtesy. If employees are arriving from another country or even from another region of the U.S., Elite Corporate Housing staffers go out of their way to give renters an overview of the area. This ensures that new residents feel safe and comfortable, which allows them greater focus for their work.

Because of its first-class service and customer focus, Elite Corporate Housing has established a loyal client base. And true to Morris County, that base is growing at a rapid clip. ☐

Rockefeller Group Development Corporation

From a business park nestled within 684 wooded acres in Morris County, to an office tower rising up in Midtown Manhattan, Rockefeller Group Development Corporation (RGDC) knows how to deliver customized, high-quality real estate for prominent companies in the U.S.

RGDC is a national real estate owner and developer, providing building space for a diverse roster of multinational companies for more than 30 years. Clients include AT&T, BASF Corporation, BMW, Unilever Cosmetics International, Continental Insurance, Federal Express, Ford Motors, Lucent Technologies, Seiko Corporation, Wells Fargo Corporation, and others.

The International Trade Center is a Rockefeller Group Development Corporation project in Mount Olive Township, Morris County, New Jersey.

In Morris County, RGDC has three development projects: Rockefeller Group Corporate Park in Florham Park, the International Trade Center (ITC) in Mount Olive, and ITC South.

The Rockefeller Group Corporate Park is located on 140 acres within Florham Park. The campus-like setting can host up to 825,000 square feet of office facilities. Among current tenants is AT&T, which chose the location for its 400,000-square-foot research and development center.

"Rockefeller Group Corporate Park is being developed in one of the most prestigious suburban office markets in the New York-Metropolitan area," says Gene Preston, vice president of development for RGDC. "In Northern New Jersey, new office building space is extremely limited. Rockefeller Group Corporate Park enables us to fill that need and create signature addresses for distinctive companies."

A second RGDC project is the ITC in Mount Olive. This 7-million-square-foot, build-to-suit business park houses about 6,200 employees who work for more than 30 companies. About a dozen multinational companies benefit from the designated New Jersey Foreign Trade Zone within the ITC.

The ITC resides next to one of the largest state parks in New Jersey. The master plan "allows for responsible economic development to move forward, while preserving and enhancing the natural beauty of the surrounding environment," says Leslie E. Smith Jr., senior vice president, development, RGDC.

Along with responsibility for the environment, community responsibility is visible as well. "As corporate citizens of Morris County, we have always made facilities at the ITC available to the community," says Smith. "We've created and continue to sponsor an annual ITC triathlon that benefits the New Jersey Special Olympics and created soccer fields for Mount Olive schools on our undeveloped land." Additionally, crowds flock to the center for an annual trade show featuring local merchants.

A third Morris County project, ITC South, is proposed adjacent to the ITC and includes plans for an 836,000-square-foot retail center.

Outside of New Jersey, RGDC's development projects include 745 Seventh Avenue in Manhattan, a 1-million-square-foot office tower being co-developed with Morgan Stanley Dean Witter & Co.; and a 2-million-square-foot industrial park and foreign trade zone in Homestead, Florida.

RGDC is one of four operating companies that make up The Rockefeller Group, a leading developer, owner, and manager of office facilities and other types of commercial real estate. The Rockefeller Group's roots can be traced to the development of one of the most famous urban business and entertainment complexes—Rockefeller Center.

Along with RGDC, other companies within The Rockefeller Group include Cushman & Wakefield Inc., Rockefeller Group Telecommunications Inc., and Rockefeller Center Business Centers Inc. □

The Rockefeller Group Corporate Park is a Rockefeller Group Development Corporation project in Florham Park, Morris County, New Jersey.

Photo by L. A. Popp.

12

Business, Finance, and the Professions

Photo by Pat McDonogh.

McKinsey & Company

No one hires McKinsey & Company to preserve the status quo. McKinsey's commitment, its passion, is helping its clients achieve positive change. It is a calling that this firm has followed since its founding 75 years ago, when it created the profession of management consulting itself.

McKinsey's 6,000 consultants serve their clients from a network of 82 offices in 43 countries. Although each location has its own personality, every site operates with a "one firm" philosophy. That means that regardless of their geographical location, McKinsey clients have access to a global network of top-notch talent and resources.

One of McKinsey's fastest growing offices is in Florham Park. The office opened in 1993 with 17 people, and today is home to 140 consultants who are as diverse and dynamic as their work. "Our consultants possess a range of valuable skills that enable them to address the unique situations that occur within the pharmaceutical, chemical, telecommunications, consumer, and other industries that flourish in Morris County," says Michael Patsalos-Fox, a director who oversees the Florham Park office. "We strategically knit together teams so that they can best collaborate with senior management on strategic issues, such as growth, licensing and acquisition, organization building, and operational improvement."

From a client's perspective, McKinsey brings a unique depth and breadth of industry-specific and functional knowledge to solving tough, ambiguous, and business-shaping problems for its clients. The firm bases its approach on structure and logic and a unique ability to draw out key strategic analyses from the facts that its consultants develop.

No matter how well versed a McKinsey consultant is in the specifics of a particular industry or function, he or she will analyze problems from a top management perspective. The firm develops its consultants' abilities to deliver such insights through stringent recruiting, years of apprenticeship in specific industries and functions, and rigorous coaching and evaluation. The quality of McKinsey's people is as important as the validity of its problem-solving expertise and business principles.

"Our consultants are looked upon as an organization's most trusted external advisor on critical issues," says Chris Simon, a McKinsey principal and one of the original 17 who opened McKinsey's New Jersey office. "We have an unbelievably rich talent pool here in New Jersey and all around the world. As a result, we have a legacy of helping clients achieve substantial, positive, and lasting change."

Michael Patsalos-Fox, Director.

McKinsey serves companies 100 years old and 100 days old. Worldwide, the bulk of McKinsey's clients are large companies, including 100 of the 150 top global companies. The firm's 1,000-plus clients also include emerging growth companies, high-tech start-ups, and family-owned enterprises. McKinsey's work with governments and institutions around the world has helped reshape entire cultures; its *pro bono* work with nonprofit organizations has helped restore individual lives.

A Remarkable Footprint

In 1926, James O. McKinsey founded McKinsey & Company in Chicago. His distinct approach to working side-by-side with senior management to solve major business problems quickly raised the credibility of the consulting field. After his death in 1937, Marvin Bower stepped up as leader of the then-small firm. Bower raised standards of professionalism, performance, and client focus to new heights and built McKinsey's future upon them.

In the years that followed, McKinsey consultants had an enduring impact on some of the most visible organizations and areas of the world. McKinsey designed the original organization of NASA; developed the Universal Product Code; advised on restoring and re-integrating East Germany's economy after the fall of the Berlin Wall; and led the first study examining Russia's economy from the ground up.

"We've built a strong reputation for helping clients chart their future and make significant improvements in their performance," says Bruno Holthof, principal. "We attribute our successful reputation to the exceptionally talented people on the McKinsey team."

The Power of Its People

More than 10,000 people worldwide make up the McKinsey team, including 800 principals (junior partners) and directors (senior partners) who privately own the company.

Statistics tell only half the story, however. A closer look at the McKinsey team reveals an extraordinary collection of cultural diversity, intellectual capital, and expertise. McKinsey's 6,000 consultants represent more than 80 different nationalities. While their academic and professional backgrounds vary widely, their individual records of accomplishment are uniformly strong.

"We search the best educational institutions, from business schools to law schools to Ph.D. programs, to find the most talented people out there," says Rick Schlesinger, principal. "We look for highly motivated people who have analytical skills, interpersonal skills, and the potential to be influential leaders in the business community."

McKinsey is the largest single employer of Rhodes scholars and Marshall scholars in the world, after the U.S. government. About 55 percent of McKinsey consultants hold an MBA degree. Of the remainder, most have advanced degrees in fields such as law, medicine, economics, science, and engineering.

MBAs at top business schools repeatedly rate McKinsey as the "ideal" employer above all other companies, and McKinsey is consistently ranked as the "most prestigious" and "most desired" company within professional services.

The firm's management thinking is often published in prominent publications such as *The Wall Street Journal, Harvard Business Review*, and *Financial Times*. Many of McKinsey's consultants are authors of leading business and management books.

"Our worldwide reputation and the kind of work we do have enabled us to attract remarkable people," says Hari Mahadevan, associate. "This is one of the very few places where a person can work on top-line issues with senior executives and influence organizations at the boardroom level."

To nurture professional development, McKinsey encourages a collegial and collaborative environment and makes unprecedented investments in developing people. For example, the Florham Park office is one of the "receiving" offices for the firm's EMERALD (Emerging Market Early Remote Associate Learning and Development) program. The program was set up to ensure that team members from every McKinsey office possess the same standards of excellence. "In certain areas of the world, McKinsey's demand for top talent exceeds the local talent pool. Through the EMERALD program, new recruits are trained for about a year at an office that is well-established and then return to their home countries," says Jurgen Wilms, director. "Not only does the program benefit the emerging markets, but it also benefits the receiving office. It gives our office a high level of cultural diversity, and it broadens our network of contacts and resources when we are looking for new solutions for our clients."

The depth of experience the consultants gain at McKinsey often opens the door to new leadership opportunities. McKinsey's alumni network includes 70 CEOs and presidents of Fortune 500 and Global Fortune 500 companies and more than 1,500 entrepreneurs who have founded or co-founded businesses. Although consultants may choose to leave McKinsey to begin new adventures, they maintain a strong connection with the firm. More than 10,000 former consultants in 70 countries belong to the firm's alumni community—a dynamic professional network of business, government, and community leaders who share knowledge and maintain relationships.

McKinsey focuses on improving client performance in a meaningful and visible way. Its success is reflected in the growing and enduring relationships with clients. Today, nearly 80 percent of the firm's work is for clients served previously.

The Clients It Serves

McKinsey serves a diverse clientele, including clients in the automotive, banking and securities, chemicals, electric power and natural gas, media and entertainment, petroleum, retail, telecommunications, and other industries.

In New Jersey, where a number of top pharmaceutical companies have headquarters, 70 percent of McKinsey's work is in health care, ranging from pharmaceutical to medical diagnostics to biotechnology companies.

"McKinsey is particularly attracted to the health-care industry because it is an industry built around helping people," says Mike Pearson, director and global head of the Pharmaceuticals and Medical Products practice. It is also an industry faced with a number of significant issues including consolidation, research and development productivity, and legislative changes that could affect the way health care is delivered and paid for. "McKinsey is the ideal partner for health-care companies because we have the knowledge and the network to help them address these issues and, ultimately, ensure that individuals receive appropriate health care," Pearson says.

How McKinsey Works

No matter how many far-flung McKinsey teams are at work around the world, the firm's consultants are united by a mission of uncompromising client service. "We routinely set, and strive to surpass, extraordinarily high performance standards in serving clients, a characteristic that sets us apart from other consulting firms," says Judith Hazlewood, principal. "McKinsey consultants don't hesitate to speak their minds because we are convinced that our clients are best served by objective, independent insights. No matter how demanding the situation, our consultants will always place the client's interests before the firm's own commercial interests."

Because McKinsey is privately owned and governed by its partners, it remains completely independent of the interests of outside shareholders or other groups that could influence its mission of client service. This independence and objectivity allows McKinsey to remain answerable only to its clients and the firm.

What is it like to work with McKinsey on a day-to-day basis? Two or three partners head each consulting team, plan the assignments, work closely with client management, and bear responsibility for the quality of the final result. The team gathers and analyzes information, formulates and tests hypotheses, develops and communicates recommendations, and prepares for implementation.

Throughout the entire process, McKinsey consultants seek to work jointly with clients, not for them. "We strive to have clients participate on teams because working together in a collaborative arrangement provides one of the most important benefits the firm can bring to a client," says David Hoffmeister, director. "Experience shows that when clients work with McKinsey study teams they can multiply the productivity of our own consultants, reduce client costs, and enhance the likelihood of effective implementation."

Similarly, the chemicals industry is facing massive changes, spurred mostly by increased global competition. "In the chemicals industry, leaders recognize that they need new ways of doing business in a dramatically changing environment," says Hoffmeister. "They are looking for new ways of thinking, which is exactly what McKinsey can offer."

Traditionally, the problems that McKinsey helps solve for many of the world's top companies are focused on strategy and organization—areas of concern for an organization's chief executive, senior officers, board members, or managing committees. The firm has deep expertise in an assortment of functional areas, such as corporate finance, globalization, marketing, and operational effectiveness, to name a few.

Increasingly, the firm is called upon to help design businesses, carry out new processes, and implement existing strategy. In the technology arena, the firm's extensive network of third-party technology vendors and professional services firms ensure that clients are able to build Internet businesses quickly. Today, McKinsey has more than 500 people engaged in e-commerce and creating e-business, either for start-ups or existing clients, such as insurance companies and banks. The firm has also established a growing global network of "Business Accelerators," where teams provide hands-on Internet business-building services.

While the bulk of McKinsey's work is in the private sector, it also advises government agencies, development organizations, and other nonprofit institutions. It assists philanthropic, civic, and cultural organizations, often on a *pro bono* basis. "We approach our *pro bono* work with the same degree of dedication and with the identical teams used with our paying clients," says Schlesinger. McKinsey dedicates about five percent of its professional hours to *pro bono* work. In New Jersey, McKinsey helps nonprofit youth organizations in urban areas run their operations more effectively and more visibly in the community. Locally and globally, the firm takes on projects that support hospitals, particularly those that help long-term-care patients, such as those with AIDS.

The Legacy Continues

For more than 70 years, McKinsey has served as a trusted external counselor on the critical issues that senior business managers face. Through some of the most jarring economic and business changes over that period, the firm has relied on its core strengths and unwavering focus on client service to analyze, adapt, and anticipate the next wave of change. Tackling the "next big thing" has always stirred McKinsey, whether it was the rise of a new corporate model, the vista of globalization, the dynamics of emerging markets, or the dawn of the digital e-commerce age.

Although its work has evolved to meet the needs of the ever-changing global business environment, McKinsey's mission remains steadfast: to help clients make substantial and lasting improvements in their performance, and to build a firm that is able to attract and develop exceptional people—people who will become inspiring leaders, and who in turn will inspire the leaders who will shape tomorrow's business and economic landscape. □

Morris County Chamber of Commerce

The corporate landscape in Morris County includes a rich roster of brilliant scientists, engaging entrepreneurs, innovative technologists, and rousing retailers. The scope of their businesses, skill sets, products, and services differ dramatically, but their day-to-day challenges often ring familiar.

Seated in the Assembly Chamber on September 14, the Leadership Morris Class of 2000 was addressed by Assemblyman Alex DeCroce (R-26) on the workings of the legislature.

"Networking with other businesspeople is one of the most effective ways to overcome challenges. We have a wealth of experience and resources in Morris County. Our mission is to make sure that businesses, regardless of size or sales, have opportunities to tap that pool of expertise and grow because of it," says William Donnelly, President of the Morris County Chamber of Commerce.

The Morris County Chamber of Commerce is a business organization dedicated to improving economic and civic life in the county. With more than 800 members representing about 135,000 employees, the Chamber is able to bring diverse businesspeople together and connect them with the information and resources they need to grow their organizations, sustain their leadership, and prepare for the future.

Donnelly and his staff are deeply engrained in the business community, aggressively identifying areas where organizations need help, and tailoring programs and services to address those needs. "Businesses are faced with tremendous change. They struggle with cultural changes that result from mergers, the introduction of new technology, legislation that impacts business, and evolving expectations from employees. The Chamber is a resourceful partner through it all," says Donnelly. "Whether you are part of a small landscaping business or a multi-billion dollar high-tech company, one of the best business decisions you can make is to be active in the Chamber."

Each year, the Chamber offers more than 50 programs and services that feature the latest business thinking to help leaders manage even the most complicated issues. For example, for more than 10 years, the Chamber has hosted Leadership Morris, a prestigious 10-month program focused on community education, community trusteeship, and business networking. More than 250 people have graduated from the program.

Another popular Chamber program is Good Morning, Morris! This bi-monthly educational and networking breakfast often draws as many as 180 people.

One of the Chamber's newest events is the Business Card Draw, which features a mini-seminar, usually about an issue in the workplace, and allows participants to promote their businesses. Attendees place their business cards in a container, five of the cards are drawn, and those individuals get to talk about their products and services during the program.

Other networking and training programs include Morris after Hours, an event with other chambers; the Great Taste of Morris, where area restaurants promote their signature dishes; Coffee with the President forums, featuring Presidents' dialogue between Chamber management and the membership; and the annual Business and Technology Trade Show.

A calendar filled with timely and provocative programs ensures there is something of value for every type of business, from start-ups to retail companies to Fortune 500s. Past topics have included "The Seven Worst Mistakes You Can Make in Investing," "Grief in the Workplace," and "Using the Web to Improve Your Business Effectiveness."

The Chamber also offers targeted committees for young professionals, small business owners, business technology professionals, and many more specialty groups.

William Donnelly, president of the Morris County Chamber of Commerce, and Arthur Gordon, director of Membership Development, are shown attending a recent meeting with a delegation from China, which included representatives from the business and government sectors. The meeting was held at the Chamber's Conference Center in Morristown.

Face-to-face programs are ideal for networking, but Donnelly and his team realize that in a thriving area like Morris County, other forms of communication are valuable, too. The Chamber offers ChamberWorks, a monthly insert to the Star-Ledger, the state's largest newspaper; hosts a half-hour ChamberWorks television show on Cablevision, RCN, Comcast, and the College of Saint Elizabeth once a week; and posts news and upcoming events on its Web site, which includes an on-line directory of Chamber members and links to their Web sites.

How is the Chamber able to offer so many effective programs and services? For starters, it has been an integral part of the business community for more than 80 years. The Chamber began as the Morristown Chamber of Commerce, but as the county became a magnet for corporate headquarters, the Chamber quickly broadened its reach. Today, the Chamber operates headquarters from a 4,500-square-foot facility in Morristown and hosts its events at a variety of sites across the county.

In addition to its historical presence, the Chamber is able to offer targeted programs because its staff members are "highly knowledgeable about the business climate," says Donnelly, who served as an attorney with Warner-Lambert (now Pfizer) for 23 years before taking the helm at the Chamber in 1995.

"We also recognize the importance of building relationships with local and state government to make sure that we provide comprehensive opportunities for our members." For instance, in 1991 on the heels of the stock market crash and recession, the Chamber partnered with the Morris County Freeholders to form a public-private entity, the Morris Area Development Group (MADG), to retain and attract business to the area. MADG developed the first CD-ROM on economic development for the state and recently created an economic growth fund in partnership with the New Jersey Economic Development Authority and nine area banks to offer Morris County businesses low-cost loans.

Members of the Morris County Chamber of Commerce's Business Technology Committee present informative and educational seminars on various aspects of doing business over the Internet. Presenters and sponsors have included: from left, Jim Lenskold, Lenskold Marketing Group; John Reiling, AcroVision Business Systems; Ann Tobias, Intara, Inc.; John Ombaldo, Masterpiece Media Design; Susan Fierro, Intara, Inc.; and Jean Yves Durocher, Consultimate.

The Chamber also contributes to the community through the Business and Education Together Foundation, Inc. (BET), a non-profit organization founded by the Chamber and funded by the state, private foundations, and companies. BET works to improve the quality of the current and future workforce. BET sponsors Understanding American Business, a summer institute for high school students; Understanding American Business for Teachers; and professional development and training programs for students, designed to prepare the workforce of the 21st century.

Donnelly says the slate of learning opportunities will continue to flourish to meet the changing business needs in Morris County. In the future, the Chamber plans to deliver more services on the Web and offer a series of discount services to help businesses reduce operational costs.

"Participation in the Chamber can help you grow your business, expand your customer base, and gain professional knowledge," says Donnelly. "The Chamber accomplishes collectively what no one business can do alone." □

Jay Kosminsky, Pfizer, Inc., is pictured with the winners of the 2000 Small Businessperson of the Year Awards at the Economic Outlook Luncheon, which was held on October 25, 2000, at Headquarters Plaza Hotel in Morristown. Dr. John Tesoriero, executive director of the New Jersey Commission on Science and Technology, was the keynote speaker at the event, which was sponsored by Pfizer and the *Daily Record*. From left: Kosminsky; Len Muscarella, Interactive Media Associates; William Donnelly, Morris County Chamber of Commerce; Joe Lunin, Pitney, Hardin, Kipp, & Szuch; Michael Kaufman, Cox Stationers & Printers; Paul Monacelli, ADP/Statewide Insurance Agencies, Inc.; Denise Smith, the *Daily Record*; and John Rothstein, Rothstein & Zuckerman, P.C.

Hilton Parsippany

It's early Monday morning, and staff members at the Hilton Parsippany are reviewing the events for the week: A presidential candidate arrives on Tuesday; an annual sales conference starts Wednesday; a pharmaceutical company hosts its associates meeting on Thursday; a birthday bash for a 100-year-old woman takes place on Friday; and a tour of Midwest college students arrives on Saturday.

It's a typical week at the Hilton Parsippany, where more than 110,000 business and weekend travelers stay each year, and thousands more attend special events and conferences.

"The Hilton delivers simple elegance," says John Loconto, general manager. "Our clients know that whether they are dining with us, staying in our guest rooms, or attending a business conference, they will receive dependable and consistent services every time."

The Hilton's commitment to service in Morris County began in 1981, when the Hilton Parsippany was built at the crossroads of Interstate 287 and Route 10. It was the first full-service major chain hotel in the area and was a welcome refuge for travelers, businesses, and families looking for a stylish, yet cost effective, place to stay and hold events.

Recently, the Hilton completed a $10-million renovation project that revitalized every area of the facility, including the 510 guest rooms and the atrium lounge—a quiet lobby bar designed for casual conversation, cocktails, light dining, business entertaining, or for watching key sporting events.

"We've incorporated richer, lighter textures throughout the hotel to provide a softer appearance," says Loconto. "The renovation project has allowed us to improve the ambience of the hotel, as well as improve the services we offer our clients." As examples, the hotel now offers a full-service business center, open six days a week, and an upgraded fitness center, including an indoor pool, that is open 18 hours daily.

Every guest room and suite within the hotel has new furniture, wallpaper, carpeting, window treatments, and lighting. Rooms contain numerous amenities, such as hairdryers, automated voice mail, two phones and data ports, high speed internet access, and coffee makers—all designed to make the guest's stay as comfortable and convenient as possible.

Because the hotel is only 25 minutes from Newark International Airport and 30 miles from New York City, domestic tour groups often enjoy the Hilton's facilities and appreciate the accomodating staff. The hotel also draws clients from many of the nearby Fortune 500 companies' headquarters, such as AT&T, IBM, Prudential Insurance, Pfizer Pharmaceuticals, and many more. "The Hilton Parsippany offers corporate, leisure, or group travelers the best accommodations and personalized service in the area," says Loconto.

Along with corporations, a variety of groups and associations have hosted major events within the hotel's 27,000 square feet of conference and banquet space, such as the New Jersey Federation of Women's Clubs, the New Jersey Press Association, and the U.S. Marine Corp. The 10,000-square-foot Grand Ballroom can accommodate up to 900 people for weddings, bar mitzvahs, corporate parties, or political and charitable fundraisers, and can seat up to 1,200 people for auditorium-style events.

Twenty-three meeting rooms come in all shapes and sizes to accommodate large conference sessions to board meetings and anything in between.

Guests at the hotel have access to heated indoor and outdoor pools, walking and jogging trails, and tennis, volleyball, and basketball courts. Laundry and valet services are available, as well as car rental services, room service, a gift shop, and a complimentary campus business shuttle service.

"We play host to some of the world's most discerning travelers," says Bill Andreorio, director of hotel sales. "It's our goal to provide them with the best experience possible, whether they are here for a few hours or a few days."

The Hilton Parsippany features two restaurants: The Harvest, for casual dining for breakfast, lunch, dinner, and Sunday brunch, and Ruth's Chris Steakhouse, open for dinner daily and recognized for serving the finest in prime-steaks, chops, and seafood. There is also Pizza Hut pizza available through room service.

The Hilton Parsippany, catering to the needs of Morris County residents, visitors, and businesses since 1981, recently completed an extensive renovation project that makes it even more indispensable to the area's hospitality industry. In addition to its 510 guest rooms and 23 meeting rooms, the Hilton offers its guests a wide array of luxuries and conveniences that would make anyone comfortable whether working or relaxing by the pool.

About 325 full- and part-time staff members ensure that the Hilton operates without a hitch. "This is a wonderful hotel with capable, committed staff," says Andreorio. "And our enthusiasm extends to the community as well."

The hotel and its staff are often hosts to major fundraising events. It's not uncommon to see a WalkAmerica kick-off party for the March of Dimes being hosted at the Hilton, or to see a luxury car being raffled off in the parking lot to raise funds for charitable organizations. Non-profit groups that help young people lead healthier and better lives frequently benefit from the Hilton's community outreach programs. Hilton-sponsorship involving golf tournaments and receptions bring in thousands of dollars and new volunteers for youth organizations like DayTop, which helps young adults and their families overcome drug and alcohol dependence, and Shepherds of Youth, which serves needy children.

Loconto explains, "This is where we work, but it's also our community. We call this home." □

Gogel Enterprises

In a sunny kitchen in 1961, Phil Gogel began to build his dream—a business selling spark plugs, batteries, and tires. Phil's space was small, but his ideas were big. Soon, his cache of automobile accessories spilled into his garage.

Gogel Tire & Automotive Center is one of several successful businesses housed at Gogel Enterprises' 26,000-square-foot facility on Route 10 East.

"Within a year, Dad's business had outgrown the house, so he moved into a gas station in Whippany and opened the tire and service center," says Howard Gogel. "My brother Stewart and I helped out when we could, pumping gas, waiting on customers. I can remember going with Dad to the local diner for bacon and egg sandwiches in the morning and listening to him talk about his plans."

The business continued to thrive, and in 1966, Phil moved the tire and service center to a larger site on Route 10, just three doors down from the current building.

Phil passed away in 1994, but not before seeing his boys grow up and his business blossom. Today, Howard and Stewart are co-owners of Gogel Enterprises, which boasts 100 employees, a 26,000-square-foot facility on Route 10 East, and several businesses, including Gogel Tire & Automotive Center, East Hanover Auto/Van Rentals, East Hanover Auto Sales, My Limousine Service, East Hanover Auto Detailing, and Ziggy's Transport & Towing.

Gogel Tire & Automotive Center is listed as one of the top 100 retail tire stores in the country. Sales and service continue to rise. "Cars last so much longer today, some as long as 200,000 miles, and they require more repairs," says Stewart.

East Hanover Auto/Van Rentals began with three cars in 1980. Today, there are 300, including 15-passenger vans and conversion vans equipped with beds and VCRs. "We recently had a woman rent a convertible for a month for her husband's 50th birthday," says Howard.

Customers can also buy all makes and models of pre-owned vehicles through East Hanover Auto Sales.

My Limousine Service includes 60 vehicles, from stretch limousines to 29-passenger shuttle buses. Chauffeurs make about 73,000 trips a year, covering nearly 4 million miles.

East Hanover Auto Detailing offers full detailing—shampoo, wax, touch up paint, and even odor elimination.

The newest member of Gogel Enterprises is Ziggy's Transport & Towing, a 24-hour service acquired in 1998. "The towing service complements our other businesses," says Stewart.

He adds that the ability to adapt and respond to a changing automobile market has helped make Gogel Enterprises a mainstay in East Hanover.

The business that once began with spark plugs scattered across a kitchen table now includes mechanics, dispatchers, chauffeurs, and others, who, the Gogels say, are responsible for the company's long-term success. "We've helped them build their homes and families, and they've helped us build a business." □

From Corvettes to vans, drivers can rent all makes and models of automobiles at East Hanover Auto/Van Rentals.

DEL MAURO, DIGIAIMO & KNEPPER, P.C.

As counsel seeking to achieve the highest level of specialization in their chosen fields, the attorneys at Del Mauro, DiGiaimo & Knepper, P.C., have worked relentlessly to develop a reputation unsurpassed by any other firm in the jurisdictions where they practice. Del Mauro, DiGiaimo & Knepper is a boutique firm with a concentration in litigation and client counseling concerning employment practices and employee benefits. The firm is thoroughly proficient in the application of the Employee Retirement Income Security Act, Age Discrimination in Employment Act, Older Workers Benefits Protection Act, Americans with Disabilities Act, Title VII of the Civil Rights Act of 1964, Family and Medical Leave Act, Conscientious Employee Protection Act, the New Jersey Law Against Discrimination and other state and federal statutory and common law pertaining to the employer/employee relationship. Backed by its vast experience representing many of the nation's leading life, health, and disability insurers as well as other businesses and organizations within the state, Del Mauro, DiGiaimo & Knepper is currently seeking to broaden its representation of employers and ERISA plans in Morris County and the surrounding area.

Inspired by a genuine enjoyment for the highly specialized areas of law in which they practice, the attorneys and staff at Del Mauro, DiGiaimo & Knepper are enthusiastic, eager, and aggressive in the representation and defense of their clients throughout the region. The firm's confidence in their abilities is fully supported by their list of qualifications, experience, and their devotion to certain well-defined areas of practice. The unmatched value of the firm's representation is also characterized by the unsurpassed savings to its clients in terms of legal costs and expenses simply by virtue of its attorneys' concentration in their chosen fields. An uncompromising standard of excellence coupled with aggressive and highly cost-efficient representation is the hallmark of the firm.

Del Mauro, DiGiaimo & Knepper's devotion to servicing its clients and maintaining its high standard of excellence is demonstrated in part by its periodic publication of newsletters and updates. These inform clients and friends of recent developments in law relevant to the firm's practice areas and jurisdictions. The firm's attorneys also serve as frequent speakers and contributing authors to various organizations including the Employment Law Committee; the Life, Health, Disability Insurance, and ERISA Committee of the Defense Research Institute; the Tort and Insurance Practices Section of the American Bar Association; and the Eastern Claims Conference, which is held annually in New York City. Attorneys in the firm are also active members and contributing authors and speakers within local organizations including the Morris County Chamber of Commerce. These activities serve the purpose of educating the firm's clients, at the firm's expense, with respect to existing law so that litigation strategies can be jointly formulated at the outset of a contested matter in the most effective and cost-efficient manner.

The firm enjoys an "AV" rating in the nationally renowned Martindale-Hubbell Directory of Lawyers/Law Firms, which is the highest possible rating bestowed in the directory and is based upon input from fellow members of the bar and judges. Del Mauro, DiGiaimo & Knepper is also recognized in Best's Directory of Recommended Insurance Attorneys and Adjusters. The firm's clients are invariably and genuinely appreciative of the extraordinary cost efficiency and high-quality legal representation provided by the firm. □

Pictured, from left: Back row: Steven P. Del Mauro, Peter J. Heck, Robert P. Lesko. Front row: Randi F. Knepper, Louis P. DiGiaimo.

Jackson, Lewis, Schnitzler & Krupman

As litigation costs rise, so does the need for preventive strategies that protect employers from potential lawsuits.

"We are highly skilled employment and labor lawyers with a focus on prevention," says Richard Schey, the managing partner of the Morristown, New Jersey, office of Jackson Lewis—a law firm recognized as a pioneer in the concept of preventive employee relations. "We work with employers to establish sound policies and practices that help them avoid workplace-related problems rather than react to them."

Vincent Cino (left) manages the litigation department at Jackson Lewis. Richard Schey (right) is the managing partner.

Founded more than 40 years ago, Jackson Lewis is one of the nation's fastest growing law firms that focuses exclusively on representing management on workplace issues. The firm has 20 offices across the country, including a Morristown office across the street from the county courthouse.

Nationwide, over 320 Jackson Lewis attorneys have experience in all aspects of workplace law, including employment litigation; affirmative action; race, gender, and age discrimination; sexual harassment; preventive labor relations; union avoidance; strikes; collective bargaining; grievance arbitration; employee leaves; pension and benefits administration; immigration; wage and hour issues; independent contractors and contingent workers; occupational safety and health; substance abuse and drug testing; employment-related electronic communication issues; employee privacy; disability rights; workplace violence; restrictive covenants and non-compete agreements; and alternative dispute resolution.

"Much of the litigation against corporations today involves employment disputes," says Schey. "We represent almost every industry and every size business—from family-owned to Fortune 100 companies—to help them create policies and procedures that promote constructive employee relations."

And when complaints arise, Jackson Lewis attorneys have extensive litigation experience. For example, in employment litigation in the past five years, the firm has defended more than 4,000 cases across the country related to such issues as discrimination, sexual harassment, and wage-hour violations.

In New Jersey alone, the firm has represented employers in more than 750 workplace-related lawsuits in the last five years. "There is a huge and diverse employee population across many different companies in New Jersey. Additionally, our state has many complex laws protecting employee rights, and employers must demonstrate the highest level of compliance possible or face costly consequences," says Vincent Cino, the head of the Morristown office's litigation department.

Because of the firm's size and national network of offices, Schey says, "our attorneys have a national perspective as well as a keen understanding of the nuances of regional business and legal environments." The regional offices offer "a relaxed, collegial atmosphere where attorneys serve as a valuable resource to the business community." For instance, in New Jersey, Jackson Lewis sponsors an annual labor and employment law symposium. The firm also sponsors conferences for labor and employment lawyers within corporate legal departments. The firm's attorneys are also active participants in the American Bar Association and the New Jersey Bar Association. □

Jackson Lewis attorneys litigate in every courthouse in New Jersey, including the Morris County Courthouse (pictured in background).

Sandler Sales Institute

How does a company turn its sales slump into success? Just ask Kathleen Szpakowski and her high-powered team of sales professionals at Sandler Sales Institute.

Since 1992, Szpakowski and her team of trainers and consultants have been helping companies evaluate their sales organizations, change cultural and individual behaviors, and accelerate growth.

"Our services are geared to those businesses that have a vision for growth and understand that the way to achieve that vision is through the ongoing development of their people," says Szpakowski. "We help companies evaluate their people and then develop and maintain a training process that will produce sustainable, measurable results."

Szpakowski's business is a branch of the internationally known Sandler Sales Institute, which is made up of privately owned franchises. Szpakowski owns and operates Sandler Sales Institute offices in Florham Park and Lawrenceville.

Her own successful sales career began in the telecommunications industry more than 20 years ago, and Szpakowski has been helping companies achieve and exceed their sales goals ever since. For example, prior to owning Sandler Sales Institute, Szpakowski is credited with building a sales organization for a telecommunications company that increased revenue 300 percent during a four-year period.

The Sandler Sales Institute in Florham Park and Lawrenceville relies on several trainers, who view themselves as "corporate behavior specialists." They have worked with small- to mid-sized companies across over 100 different industries, as well as partnered with executives from major corporations to help them improve the effectiveness of their sales management teams. It's not unusual to find Sandler trainers working within the software industry one day and a chemical company the next, or mixing fun and sharing ideas for best practices with clients at a local horseracing event.

Szpakowski explains, "We're not recruiters," although she has a network of recruitment resources she often shares with clients. "We are change agents who help companies identify the behaviors that have the highest impact on their sales, make sure that recruiters are interviewing people based on those behaviors, and provide training that supports and develops those behaviors."

Kathleen Szpakowski, owner and operator of Sandler Sales Institute offices in Florham Park and Lawrenceville.

Although the ultimate goal is the same for all companies—continuous sales growth—the programs and processes for achieving that goal come in all shapes and sizes based on client needs. "From in-depth evaluations of personnel, including executive management, to private coaching of business owners, sales managers, and salespeople, our customized processes are effective and result in sales growth year after year," says Szpakowski.

To help clients target specific needs, Sandler Sales Institute has a cache of high-tech tools that generate comprehensive and candid reports. There are software programs that help sales professionals understand and build upon their unique selling styles, plus assessment applications that measure the "performance DNA" a company needs to achieve superior performance in a particular position.

Sandler Sales Institute also offers a 360-degree feedback program, which gathers information about an individual's effectiveness from several people who work with that individual. The 360-degree concept is not new, but Szpakowski says Sandler's approach is unique. "We don't put people through a one-day training program and then assume they are using the process effectively." Instead, Sandler's 360-degree assessment process includes a follow-up system to ensure results.

And results are key. "There is tremendous pressure on companies to accomplish more with less resources," says Szpakowski. "Therefore, it is more critical than ever to have the right people, with the right competencies, and the right attitude in key positions. And that's where we can help." □

A night out on the town with clients at the Meadowlands Racetrack.

TransOptions, Inc.

New Jersey commuters spend an estimated 34 extra hours a year in their cars because of traffic-clogged roadways. In addition to those wasted hours, there are extra fuel and maintenance costs to bear. "We're talking about a problem that has tremendous impact on our communities and our businesses," says John F. Ciaffone, president of TransOptions, Inc. "But there is a light at the end of the tunnel, and it's called TransOptions."

Formerly known as MCRIDES, TransOptions is a non-profit, public/private partnership created to reduce traffic congestion, improve air quality, promote options for commuting, and advocate for more effective transportation systems. The company, formed in 1986 to focus on traffic congestion in Morris County, broadened its vision to include other congested areas. Today, TransOptions serves Morris, Sussex, and Warren Counties, as well as suburban Passaic, Union, and Essex counties.

"Our role is to advocate for regional transportation options that benefit both employers and commuters," says Ciaffone. "We bring together businesses, counties, municipalities, and the state to address traffic problems and develop the best commute choices possible."

TransOptions staff members take on a variety of initiatives to improve transportation options. For starters, they promote public transit, vanpooling, and carpooling. Their efforts have resulted in 70 vanpools, 1,110 carpools and 7 commuter shuttle/WHEELS systems.

Another TransOptions success is Project:Power Commute, an innovative program that places eight electric vehicles at the Morristown Train Station for use by employees from five participating companies. "Alternative-fuel vehicles help reduce pollution that causes serious respiratory illnesses," says Ciaffone.

In addition to offering transportation alternatives, staff members gauge employee attitudes through surveys; address parking, biking, and pedestrian access issues; and help major corporations set up telecommuting and compressed work schedules. TransOptions also helps companies establish and implement alternative work schedules for their employees. This is accomplished through assisting in the development and implementation of telecommute policies and through on-site training of employers and employees.

Funding for TransOptions is provided through contributions, consulting fees, and contracts with NJDOT and NJTRANSIT. Corporate sponsors have access to many services including a computerized ride-matching service, an Emergency Ride Home program for employees, a quarterly newsletter, traffic and ozone alerts, and a commuter survival guide in both Spanish and English. TransOptions can also assist businesses in the establishment of programs, which will allow them to take advantage of tax benefits offered by federal and state laws.

The benefits of TransOptions' programs and services are numerous. Most importantly, commuter options reduce the number of cars on the road. "If everyone left a car home only one day a week, we would have 10 to 20 percent less traffic," says Ciaffone. "And fewer cars mean less congestion, increased mobility, and improved air quality.

TransOptions offers transportation alternatives that are safe and, at the same time, have a positive impact on the bottom line for business. Ciaffone reports, "our clients tell us that such options are an important employee recruitment and retention tool. Also, employees are more productive when their commute is reduced or simplified. Absenteeism is reduced, and employees arrive to work more relaxed, on time, and ready to begin the day." □

Fleet of electric vehicles from Project: Power Commute at Morristown Train Station.

Photo by L. A. Popp.

Enterprise Index

American Home Products Corporation
5 Giralda Farms
Madison, New Jersey 07940
Phone: 973-660-5000
www.ahp.com
Pages 118-119

ASCO
50-60 Hanover Road
Florham Park, New Jersey 07932
ASCO Valve, Inc.:
Phone: 800-972-ASCO
Fax: 973-966-2628
E-mail: info-valve@asco.com
ASCO Power Technologies:
Phone: 800-937-ASCO
Fax: 973-966-5709
E-mail: bphelan@asco.com
www.asco.com
Pages 100-101

BASF Corporation
3000 Continental Drive North
Mount Olive, New Jersey 07828-1234
Phone: 973-426-2600
Fax: 973-426-2610
E-mail: www.basf.com
www.basf.com
Pages 96-97

College of Saint Elizabeth
2 Convent Road
Morristown, New Jersey 07960
Phone: 973-290-4000
Admissions: 973-290-4700
Toll-free Admissions: 800-210-7900
Fax: 973-290-4710
E-mail: apply@liza.st-elizabeth.edu
www.st-elizabeth.edu
Page 110

County College of Morris
214 Center Grove Road
Randolph, New Jersey 07869
Phone: 973-328-5000
Admissions: 973-328-5100
Admissions Fax: 973-328-5199
Admissions E-mail: admiss@ccm.edu
www.ccm.edu
Pages 108-109

Daily Record
800 Jefferson Road
Parsippany, New Jersey 07054
Phone: 973-428-6200
Fax: 973-884-5048
E-mail: newsroom@dailyrecord.com
www.dailyrecord.com
Page 90

Del Mauro, DiGiaimo & Knepper, P.C.
8 Headquarters Plaza, North Tower
Morristown, New Jersey 07960
Phone: 973-292-2277
Fax: 973-292-1551
E-mail: rlesko@ddkesqs.com
www.ddkesqs.com
Page 143

DPC Cirrus Inc.
111 Canfield Avenue, B-15
Randolph, New Jersey 07869
Phone: 973-927-2828
Fax: 973-927-4101
E-mail: cscribner@dpconline.com
www.dpcweb.com
Pages 94-95

Elite Corporate Housing
P.O. Box 428
Long Valley, New Jersey 07853
Phone: 908-813-1871
Fax: 908-813-1880
Pages 128-129

Fairleigh Dickinson University
Florham-Madison Campus
285 Madison Avenue
Madison, New Jersey 07940
Phone: 973-443-8500
Teaneck-Hackensack Campus
1000 River Road
Teaneck, New Jersey 07666
Phone: 201-692-2000
E-mail: globaleducation@fdu.edu
www.fdu.edu
Page 111

Gogel Enterprises
235 Route 10
East Hanover, New Jersey 07936
Phone: 973-428-5225
Fax: 973-428-3759
E-mail: info@mylimo.com
www.gogelauto.com
Page 142

GPU, Inc.
300 Madison Avenue
P.O. Box 1911
Morristown, New Jersey 07912-1911
Phone: 973-401-8200
www.gpu.com
Pages 88-89

Heath Village
Schooley's Mount Road
Hackettstown, New Jersey 07840
Phone: 908-852-4801
Fax: 908-852-3748
E-mail: info@heathvillage.com
www.heathvillage.com
Page 125

Hilton Parsippany
One Hilton Court
Parsippany, New Jersey 07054
Phone: 973-267-7373
Fax: 973-984-2896
www.hilton.com
Pages 140-141

Honeywell International
101 Columbia Road
Morristown, New Jersey 07962
Phone: 973-455-5876
Fax: 973-455-3632
E-mail: andre.lewis2@honeywell.com
www.honeywell.com
Page 104

Jackson, Lewis, Schnitzler & Krupman
60 Washington Street
Morristown, New Jersey 07960
Phone: 973-538-6890
Fax: 973-540-9015
www.jacksonlewis.com
Page 144

Maersk Inc.
Two Giralda Farms
Madison Avenue
Madison, New Jersey 07940
Phone: 973-514-5000
Fax: 973-514-5410
E-mail: nammktadv@maersk.com
www.maersksealand.com
Pages 102-103

McKinsey & Company
600 Campus Drive
Florham Park, New Jersey 07932
Phone: 973-549-6600
Fax: 973-549-6300
www.mckinsey.com
Pages 134-137

Morris County Chamber of Commerce
25 Lindsley Drive
Morristown, New Jersey 07960
Phone: 973-539-3882
Fax: 973-539-3960
www.morrischamber.org
Pages 138-139

Morristown Memorial Hospital—Atlantic Health System
100 Madison Avenue
Morristown, New Jersey 07962
Phone: 973-971-5000
Fax: 973-290-7010
www.atlantichealth.org
Pages 114-117

National Prescription Administrators, Inc.
711 Ridgedale Avenue
East Hanover, New Jersey 07936
Phone: 973-503-1000
Fax: 973-503-1084
E-mail: rullman@npanet.com
www.npanet.com
Pages 120-121

RFL Electronics Inc.
353 Powerville Road
Boontown Township, New Jersey 07005
Phone: 973-334-3100
Fax: 973-334-3863
E-mail: sales@rflelect.com
www.rflelect.com
Pages 98-99

Rockefeller Group Development Corporation
New Jersey Headquarters
500 International Drive North, Suite 345
Mount Olive, New Jersey 07828
Phone: 973-347-9100
Fax: 973-347-4047
E-mail: gpreston@rockgrp.com
www.rockefellergroup.com
Page 130

Saint Clare's Health Services
400 West Blackwell Street
Dover, New Jersey 07801-2525
Phone: 973-989-3124
Fax: 973-989-3195
E-mail: jsbrocco@saintclares.org
www.saintclares.org
Page 124

Sandler Sales Institute
23 Vreeland Road, Suite 108
Florham Park, New Jersey 07932
Phone: 973-966-0055
Fax: 973-514-1154
E-mail: bethebest@sandler.com
www.bethebest.sandler.com
Page 145

The Seeing Eye
P.O. Box 375
Morristown, New Jersey 07963-0375
57 Washington Valley Road
Morristown, New Jersey 07960
Phone: 973-539-4425
Fax: 973-539-0922
E-mail: semaster@seeingeye.org
www.seeingeye.org
Page 122-123

Smiths Industries Actuation Systems, Inc.
110 Algonquin Parkway
Whippany, New Jersey 07981
Phone: 973-428-9898 x200
Fax: 973-428-8532
E-mail: das@act-sys.com
www.si-act-sys.com
Page 105

TransOptions, Inc.
2 Ridgedale Avenue, Suite 200
Cedar Knolls, New Jersey 07927
Phone: 973-267-7600
Fax: 973-267-6209
E-mail: info@transoptions.org
www.transoptions.org
Page 146

ACKNOWLEDGEMENTS

The author wishes to acknowledge information obtained from the following publications:

Morris County Trends, 1998, Morris County Chamber of Commerce.
Morris County Data Book, 1998, Morris County Planning Board.

The editor wishes to acknowledge the following organizations for information obtained from their Web sites:

Chester Borough
College of Saint Elizabeth
County College of Morris
Drew University
Historic Morris Visitors Center
International Trade Center
Morris County Board of Chosen Freeholders (official Morris County site)
Morris County Park Commission
Morristown Memorial Hospital
Morristown National Historical Park
New Jersey Shakespeare Festival
Saint Clare's Health Services
The Community Theatre
The Nanticoke Lenni-Lenape Indians of New Jersey
Town of Boonton
Town of Dover
Township of Denville
Waterloo Village

The editor wishes to thank the following people who provided photographs for the book:

Angelo Carfagna, Fairleigh Dickinson University
Jeff Crowmartie and Tom Harris, Drew University
Bridget Daley, New Jersey Shakespeare Festival
Diane Zitek, County College of Morris

Photo by L. A. Popp.

Index